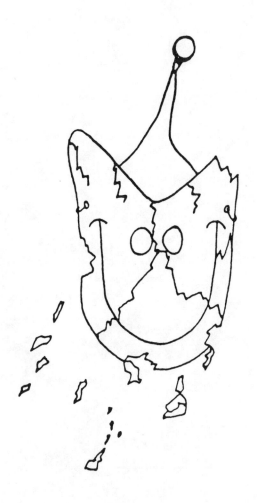

The Child
That Never Was

*Grieving Your Past
To Grow Into The Future*

Yvonne Kaye, Ph.D.

Illustrations by Daniel Sean Kaye

Health Communications, Inc.
Deerfield Beach, Florida

Yvonne Kaye, Ph.D.
22 North York Road
Willow Grove, Pennsylvania 19090
(215) 659-7110

Library of Congress Cataloging-in-Publication Data

Kaye, Yvonne
  The child that never was : grieving your past to grow into the future/
Yvonne Kaye.
      p. cm.
  Includes bibliographical references
  ISBN 1-55874-088-0
  1. Adult children of alcoholics — United States. 2. Adult children of
dysfunctional families — United States. 3. Adult children of alcoholics —
Rehabilitation — United States. 4. Adult children of dysfunctional families
— Rehabilitation — United States. 5 Self-actualization
(Psychology)   I.Title.
HV5132.K39   1991
362.29'13-dc 20   90-38589
                                                                     CIP

© 1991 Yvonne Kaye
ISBN 1-55874-088-0

Publisher: Health Communications, Inc.
                 3201 S.W. 15th Street
                 Deerfield Beach, Florida 33442

Cover design by Graphic Expressions

Dedication

To my mother — Cecelia, *in memoriam.*

To the generation most affected by my growth and change, my children: Rosanne, Michelle, Colin and Daniel, with love and respect.

To all those who have, by their encouragement, honesty and unconditional love, woven the threads, helping to create this miraculous tapestry I call my life.

With gratitude.

Yvonne Kaye

Contents

Preface

So many difficulties experienced by suffering adults are from grieving something that never was. How hard that is. Adult Child Mourners know that something is missing in their lives — but what?

I hope to make you think.

I hope to make you remember.

I hope to help you grieve what never was.

I hope to help you celebrate what is.

We Adult Child Mourners have to learn to appreciate ourselves, create our own normality, live to our potential and recognize our right to be happy.

Introduction

Many books have been published on the plight of adult children from dysfunctional families. Many of them are predicated on the premise that these parents wanted their children, but didn't know what to do with them once they arrived. The idea of these very worthy books is to help suffering adult children make peace with themselves, learn to understand the severity of the dysfunction of their parents and practice forgiveness. Some books suggest that the only way for adult children to recover from the debilitation of this syndrome is to physically recapture the childhood dream that never was and to be with their parents and family.

My hypothesis is that not all children were wanted, deserved or yearned for. Many were results of mistakes and *absolutely not wanted*. It is necessary for the adult child to face the fact, if it is so, that they were not wanted, were considered a burden, a nuisance and a thorn in the flesh. It is necessary to mourn and grieve over this realization.

The adult child will be referred to in this book as the Adult Child Mourner. This is not a problem suffered only by those raised in alcoholic families. Dysfunctions cover many varied painful childhoods. All of them are referred to in a later chapter.

This book also addresses, with rigorous honesty, the plight of the unwanted child. It acknowledges that there are different kinds of love and acceptance.

There are many reasons for unwanted children. Some are . . .

- Spontaneous sex
- Unplanned pregnancy
- Two people living only for one another
- Parent didn't like children
- Parent was from a huge family
- Parent was an only child
- Parent didn't want children
- Clash of personalities
- Child got in the way of careers
- Child hindered social, vacation, schooling plans.

Grieving the childhood that never was is complex. Not only was there no childhood, no frame of reference of what a normal childhood was, but possibly there was no love from the parents at all. Facing and accepting that cruel and stark reality releases Adult Child Mourners from the continuous search for parental love.

I constantly hear Adult Child Mourners describe their "normal" childhood years. They speak of beatings, of all kinds of abuse, of pain and anguish.

They say, in the vast majority of cases, "Don't get me wrong, Yvonne, I love my parents."

I say, "Bullshit!"

The biological connection is responsible for people's massive confusion and ultimately for *"Death By Should."*

How often do we hear this in group therapy? "My mother infuriates me. I talk to her sisters about what to do, and they say, 'You know how she is! You're her daughter; you must care for her. She was there for you.' "

The truth is, "No, she wasn't there for me," but the daughter cannot say that.

We live in the fantasy that we were wanted, planned and cared for, but that "something" happened that made it diffcult to love us. It was our fault that we were unlovable. They had so much on their minds.

This reality is so hard to accept. No one wants to believe that they were not loved. I can hear the pro-love advocates screaming, *"Heresy.* Forgiveness is the answer!"

I won't argue with the importance of forgiveness. However, forgiveness doesn't mean it is necessary to recapture the relationship. Who would really want to? Some relationships in families can be resolved as adults on an entirely different level. However, many Adult Child Mourners report that they still feel like small children in the company of their parents, particularly when they are criticized.

I believe it is important to follow every avenue to remedy past pain. We have to create a boundary so past pain does not become present pain. This only happens with a knowledge of having completed the options and reaching closure. I can still hear the screams of, "Heresy!" Parents are people who have given birth — it's simply another label. The only difference is that there is a biological connection. In translation — we put up with more from our families than we would from our friends.

Why is this? Culture, Judeo-Christian teachings and society told us to. It is time to question what is acceptable and what is unacceptable behavior.

Adult Child Mourners spend vast amounts of time struggling with love. They look for it in all the wrong places, starting with their parents.

In this book it is my goal to help the Adult Child Mourner recognize the problem and acknowledge the confusion of being lied to, cheated, abused and ignored. They can discover their adult responsibility to their own recovery and let go. To do this, they must go through the grieving process. The 12-Step Program puts it succinctly: "There is no easier, softer way." This is a pain that cannot be circumvented. It is necessary to go through it in order to release it.

The Adult Child Mourner has to deal with all kinds of memories. Each person grieves and heals differently. But we all share one thing in common — the probability of total recovery. It takes a simple commitment to ourselves of whatever it takes.

Know from the start that there is recovery: powerful, lasting, exciting, joyful and fun. There is forgiveness: relief from the blindness of blame, shame and guilt. And there is love.

Stay with me as we travel this journey from grieving to healing together, for this is also my story. I was the six-year-old

1

What Did I Do?

A child cries — silently. Who is there to listen?
A child screams — as a mime, mouthing the words.
People do not want to hear.
A child succumbs to distrust the surrounds.
Knowing of the secrets among the Big People.
The Bigs provide testament, character witness, bold,
definite.
They protect their peers against the little ones.
Denial. Most descriptive.

London, England, 1940

She stepped out into the strong sunlight, blinking against the glare. She had no idea where she was or where anyone she knew was. She had no feelings — not happy, not sad, not afraid, nothing but numbness.

1

She was a pretty child with blond hair and blue eyes, just six years old.

That morning — she didn't know how many hours ago — her mother had taken her to school, put a gas mask in a cardboard box across her shoulders and a small suitcase in her hand, herded her onto a bus with a lot of other children and simply said "Goodbye." There was no kiss, no hug, no "I love you," no explanation. There was nothing but a cold numbness of oblivion. There had been so much "leaving" in her short life, emotionally and physically, that the child was resigned to it at the age of six.

A conspiracy of silence, perhaps reflecting the fears of their parents, made children obedient in that wartime era. Not knowing how to handle crises of national importance caused panic for many people. Some sent their children away from London to keep them safe.

But a small child raised in a dysfunctional family, sent away with no explanation, could know nothing of the danger of bombs or the need for security. All she could know was that she was being rejected and abandoned, that the people she relied on no longer wanted her.

This little six-year-old decided that, because she was being sent away and Mummy was staying with Daddy, she must have been very bad indeed. Certainly the message was very clear that it was out of the question for her ever to be bad or to upset grown-ups again. At the same time, without realizing it then, she made many powerful decisions to survive the ordeal of separation. One of the most significant was that she would never allow anyone to love her again — it just hurt too much.

At this point the child did what so many do at this incredible helplessness — emotionally, she shut down. There was no one to turn to.

"I'll take that one." The voice startled her out of her reverie. She was given a shove toward a tall, silver-haired man. She put her hand in his and walked with him toward the hustle and bustle of registration tables. It was all very normal to her — she came from a dysfunctional family, where children are frequently blindly obedient to keep the peace.

Small children do not verbalize, they internalize. They are the total victims. Their lives are unmanageable by someone else's design. In her despair, this little girl made an unconscious decision to skip something very valuable — her childhood.

When a child is struggling to survive, not knowing the how, having only the instinct of the human animal, there is no time to cogitate on the whys or the wherefores. The only awareness is to make it for another day. This void, this emptiness for children, is called *grief.*

Grief is a word frequently misunderstood. Usually it is interpreted as sadness as the result of a death. However, every aspect of loss can result in grieving. In the case of Adult Children, they are in a state of grief over the childhood that never was. The pain of losing something or someone is hard to bear, be it due to death, divorce, moving away or ending a love affair. Consider the word loss.

The list of possible losses is endless:

Divorce, youth, friendship, relocation, baldness, bankruptcy, weight, sleep, vitality, virginity, voice, employment, sight, hearing, strength, virility, interest, love, amputation.

We know that loss is vast, even if we don't know whether it is final. We may comprehend that death is final. In both these areas, death and loss, there is knowledge: someone has died, something is lost. These are facts — indisputable. We know what we are mourning.

However, it is extremely difficult to mourn a situation never experienced, but desired above all: the warmth, security, joy and love of a happy childhood.

How does one deal with recovery from a situation unknown? How does an adult know what to mourn? What is a happy childhood? To people raised in a normal, healthy family, these questions may be simple; to the adult child, they are unanswerable. It is like expecting a person to understand a lecture delivered in Russian when they have never learned that language. They simply cannot comprehend what it could be. Adult children have no concept of emotions. Sadness, anger and pain are incomprehensible; numbness and fantasy are friends. When adult children state, "I don't know how I feel," they really don't know.

Adult children get lost in the utter confusion of being unable to pinpoint why their behaviors are repetitive and their relationships go sour due to some unseen source, some fear that emotionally paralyzes.

Elizabeth, a professional woman, was 40 when she came to me for help.

One of three sisters, she was the scapegoat in the family. She told me:

The atmosphere in my childhood home was stifling. There was absolute silence most of the time, especially at our "nightmare" mealtimes. I can remember my body being rigid all the time — never relaxed — always anticipating a blow from somewhere. The belt was ready whether I needed it or not. I remember hearing screams coming from a locked room where my younger sister and my parents were. I felt that whatever was happening in there was my fault, and that's what I grew up believing. I used to watch *The Brady Bunch* sometimes on television and wonder what kind of place that was. I mean, no one was ever beaten, they were listened to, and problems were resolved without bloodshed. I even found myself watching commercials showing kids who were sick and feeling amazed that those children were cuddled and cared for. My parents were furious if any one of us didn't feel well. We wouldn't dare. Happy childhood? Only on television!

Elizabeth matured into a loving, caring woman — too loving and too caring. Her relationships with men were self-punishing, both emotionally and physically. She tried to avoid conflict by keeping the peace, being accessible and rescuing her troubled lovers. Her idea of providing her children with a happy family life was to control to the nth degree what they did and who their friends were. She insisted on family outings and vacations until they married. Two of the children were still maintaining that family facade.

I shared with Elizabeth that I wasn't sure which caused more difficulty — the "none" childhood or the *Brady Bunch!* She didn't know either.

Frank, another of my clients, remembers nothing from his childhood except pain and degradation.

"Fun?" he asks. "What's that? I knew 'work' from the age of six, I knew silence and smacks in the mouth. What was more damaging was that I never quite understood what I had done to deserve such treatment."

Such treatment is a part of Frank's life today. He has been in impossible relationships with women who have taken advantage of him and continue to "smack him in the mouth" literally and take everything he offers to them. This is the way he maintains love and peace.

With both Elizabeth and Frank, as well as many of my adult child patients, I work two powerful programs:

1. To examine the levels of grieving.
2. To recognize the powerful decisions they made as small children in order to survive, and then learn to reverse those decisions.

Because those decisions are firmly entrenched at the subconscious level, a variety of treatment modalities are required to identify them. There is no particular structure or regimen that works for everyone. A very definite requirement, however, is an ability to listen unconditionally to one's own pain and to accept it. *No minimizing allowed!*

As a happy childhood is an unknown entity, my journey has been rather like detective work. Not surprisingly, I am a detective story addict. This predilection has sharpened my wits to recognize symptoms I would have overlooked in the past. On meeting a new patient, I assume they are adult children of dysfunction with the multitudinous list of symptoms available. I quickly learn exactly where the problem lies and take it from there.

"Tell me about your parents."

"What was it like at home, growing up?"

When they tell me, as they frequently do, "That's not what I came here for, and anyway I can't recall my childhood," I know we are in for a long haul of resistance, denial, protection and misguided loyalty.

Not knowing what we missed, but knowing "something" is missing, is the beginning of the process.

2

How It All Began For Me

I came from a really crazy family. "Dysfunctional" is the word we use today. My grandmother and grandfather had emigrated to England from Poland. They had 14 children, including one set of twins. One of the twins died when he was two years old and the remaining twin grew up believing that "the wrong one died." This she was led to understand from the age of two. She was impossible all of her adult life. My mother was the middle of the 13 remaining children and as perfect a codependent as ever existed.

What a mixed bag this family was. The craziness was indescribable. They either all talked to each other, nobody talked to one another or some of them talked about the others. Someone didn't, then someone did. Everybody was intervening constantly. The enabling and fixing were just incredible. Armed warfare paled in comparison.

The center of the family was a tailor shop on Brixton Hill in London. The back of it was my grandparents' huge house. My grandfather was a character who would curse in English and not know what he was saying because no one would tell him the Polish translation.

Early Years

My problems began when I was in my mother's womb. She became pregnant by a man I still know very little about. She was no young naive innocent; she was 30 years old. She didn't marry my father. For the sake of a name for me, she married someone else and proceeded to have 25 horrendous years with him.

I was born into chaos and addictions. I didn't know it as a child, but I have recently discovered that my mother was a prescription drug addict with a drinking problem. I think one of her brothers was also addicted. He certainly was an active user when he was out of prison. The major disaster for my mother was her inferiority complex and severe low self-esteem. I was her only natural child. I found out later that the man she married said she could keep me if I were a girl, but if I had been a boy, she would have had to give me up. I never did understand that, but I learned from a very young age not to ask questions. It was highly unlikely that I would ever get an answer. I was much more likely to be punished for even asking. I was very young when I stopped asking questions or at least learned to be very careful about them.

Until I was almost six, my life had some bright spots. I was the apple of my grandfather's eye. I can remember being in my grandparents' house, where there was a parrot and a greyhound. When I was put down for a nap, those two used to guard me. This is one of the few things I can remember about my early years.

My immediate family didn't have any money, although some members of the extended family were very wealthy indeed.

Because we were the poor relations and couldn't afford a vacation, the rest of the family would take us to a holiday spot in a place called Blean near Canterbury in Kent. It was a farmhouse/guesthouse and I loved it there. I loved the people. I remember some of the happiest moments of my life spent sitting at that huge farmhouse kitchen table with Mrs. Buesden and her family. They were so warm and loving. She was everything good that one would ever think a farmer's wife to be. The place was called Yew Tree Farm and it was my haven.

I must have had some recognition of what normal was at that time, to feel so comfortable there. Not for a moment, though, did I believe it could be part of my life on a permanent basis. Hurt children have wisdom well beyond their years.

The War Begins

We were at Yew Tree Farm in late August and early September of 1939. One morning, September 3rd, I remember waking up to hustle, bustle and chaos. Of course, I didn't pay too much attention to it because that was the norm for my family. There was usually someone screaming at someone else, one of the aunts yelling at one of the others.

September 3, 1939 — the day war broke out in Europe. Of course, I had no idea what was going on at that stage. I was not quite six years old and I was on holiday with my cousins. This particular morning something strange happened. People were making noise but they weren't saying anything. Bags were being packed, tears were being shed, and everyone was talking and talking and talking about nothing.

I noticed that my bags were not being packed. I was so used to being left and dumped on people that I really didn't pay too much attention. My mother would frequently forget my existence and leave me on a street corner with the groceries. Once she left me in the London Zoo. Funny what we remember!

One of my cousins said, "We're leaving."

"We are leaving?"

I couldn't make head or tail of that. I ran around asking all of the grownups, "Who's leaving? Where are you going? What's going on? What's all the noise?"

"Yvonne, everything's going to be all right." Standard answer.

That was it. That was the explanation of my parents leaving me there and my cousins and their parents returning to London.

I had heard noises on the radio of things like "war" and "Hitler" and "Chamberlain" and "conference." I just didn't pay much attention. I was not quite six years old. I was into playing and jumping on the pigs in the sties, this being a farm. I had been just generally trying to forget what it was like in London, living with my mother and her husband, instead of getting into the fun of being with my cousins.

It wasn't such an ordeal at that point, mainly because children don't have any concept of time. I had no idea how long they were away until that one day my cousins told me they were leaving and I wasn't. This seems to be the story of my life: people I love constantly leaving.

I have this thing about triangles, which in my recovery I have learned to think of as pyramids. My triangle was living with two dysfunctional people. I was right in the middle of their fights, arguments, despairs and insanity. At this point, I did not even recognize the molesting from my stepfather. In this environment I learned how to deny very well. When my mother spoke on the telephone or any of her siblings stopped by, there was no indication that anything was amiss. We were the typical secretive, looking-good family.

In a way, being in Canterbury was a relief. It was all right when my cousins were there, but my feelings of abandonment really began to take hold when they left. I had severe separation anxiety which caused me to start wetting the bed and be careless with my clothing. At times I felt invisible.

So there were no questions from me, because I knew there wouldn't be any answers. Therefore, I internalized my fears and helplessness, and out came unacceptable behavior. Because the lovely woman with whom I lived was so exasperated with this behavior, she used to threaten that if I came home from school once more in that condition, I would go straight to bed with no supper. That went on for quite a long time. I was so terrified, I was unable to control simple bodily functions. There was absolutely no sensitivity in my life at all. I really loved Mrs. Buesden, but she had no idea of the separation anxiety I was going through at that time, the pain and grief children are not supposed to have.

I celebrated my sixth birthday away from my parents at Yew Tree Farm. The world was in chaos and so was I. There was war in Europe. My whole family was disintegrating. People were going off in all different directions, telling me nothing.

Because Canterbury was close to a port, it was considered unsafe and I had to go back to London. At that point I didn't realize why I was going back. I soon discovered that the plan was to get the children out of London and ship them to Australia, America or any country that was not involved with the war at that time.

In my excitement at going back it certainly didn't occur to me that I would be sent away again, and I wouldn't have understood it anyway. Remember, I was raised in a total conspiracy of silence. I was told nothing, but just did as I was told. Most children in my generation did. It was difficult for me to understand the whole aspect of what was going on because I didn't know how to ask questions. You have to be a person to be able to do that.

On my return to London everything was in upheaval. It didn't seem to be important whether I was there or not because nobody paid any attention. Everything was discussed just as if I were not there. People didn't seem to realize that I did hear, feel and understand. It was not easy being a child in a dysfunctional family then, any more than it is today. The pain, grief and fear over "How long am I going to be able to stay here?" began to take hold.

Whether it was denial or whether it was complete unawareness, I had no idea what was going to happen. This was ambivalence and helplessness. After all these years, there are still blocks of time and people of which I have no knowledge whatsoever. It seemed to me that there was a lot of discussion going on. *But nobody talked.* Members of the family kept disappearing. Aunts and uncles took their children and went out of the city for safety.

Sent Away

Then one morning when I was ready for school, my mother put my gas mask in a brown box around my shoulders (which was common at that time) and a little suitcase in my hand. She took me to school, but instead of sending me into the building, she put me on a bus. She didn't say goodbye so I didn't pay any attention. I just thought I was going on a bus ride, a school outing. A label was put on my coat, but that wasn't uncommon. If we ever went anywhere, it was important that people knew our names.

Then the bus left. It went for a very long time, just kept going and going and going for what I now know to have been about four hours. I was so numb at this point I can't recall if anybody else asked questions. I know I completely shut down emotionally and made the decision that I would never let anybody love me again — it hurt too much to be separated so often.

I don't even remember who was on the bus. I don't remember any of my friends from that time. I don't know if they were crying, laughing or playing. I just don't recall. My earliest recollection was the bus pulling into a quaint market square in Highbridge, a small village in Somerset, in the west of England. As I got off, I can remember some of the teachers on the bus telling us to be quiet and pay attention. I stood at the steps, and a tall man with silver hair pointed to me and said, "I'll take that one."

What amazes me now is that I just went with him and didn't even think about it. I had no idea of even considering any other action. I was six years old. I didn't know where I was. I had no idea why I was there and why I was going away from home. No idea at all. Except that I was doing as I was told again. All this time, I never shed a tear. I was already a little adult.

He took me by the hand to go and register. He was a very handsome military man and a grandfather figure to me. I believe I really loved him, instantly. He was a port in a storm for me.

However, that did not compensate for the pain and grief his wife, his daughter and her friend put me through. Both he and his wife were 78 years old and his daughter and her friend were both about 45, unmarried women who were bitter and angry.

As a child I was a pretty little thing. I looked and behaved a little bit like Shirley Temple with my gold curls, singing and dancing. There was an active clown in me which compensated for the pain that I'd been in for all those six long years of life. I believe the three women all resented my looks and my clowning.

The man took me home to the house, which was a mansion to me, and introduced me to an austere lady, haughty, with her hair pulled tightly into a bun. She didn't look at me and didn't touch me but just said, "Take her upstairs and let her see her room." I can remember thinking, "My room? Why do I have a room here? I have a room at home. Why on earth would I want to have a room?"

He took me upstairs and showed me this very pretty room, and I began to get feelings of severe panic because something was wrong. My child's mind could not understand why a perfect stranger would take me to their home and give me a room. I couldn't understand that and I became very scared. In panic, there's enough strength to question. I started asking him, "Why am I here? Where is my mummy? Where is my dad? Where is my grandma?"

He said nothing. Just smiled. It seemed I was not going to get any answers from anybody. It was so terribly confusing that I simply didn't know what was going on in my life at all. Nobody was about to tell me. Then I started to cry. There was no response from him, except I can recall a heavy sigh.

Then he went downstairs. I remember sitting on that bed. I didn't cry anymore then, and it seems to me from that time I stopped crying almost completely. I still have great difficulty crying today. I was too terrified to cry. I had no idea what was going to become of me. No one was going to tell me. I sat on the bed staring at my little suitcase sitting beside me.

I heard the woman call me to go down for something to eat. I didn't want to eat. I didn't know where I was. I had no idea who these people were. Where was my mother? Why did she leave me like this and not say anything — again? Was she going to come back soon? I ran down the stairs and asked, "Where is my mother? Is she coming here soon?"

This began the fear that haunted me most of my life. It made me believe I was sent away because I had done something really bad. In treatment, I recalled that not long before

this I had told my mother her husband was molesting me.
Then I was sent away. Put that together in a small child's head.
"I must have been bad; that's why I'm sent away."

It had to be that way. My cousins had gone with their own
parents. My mother had chosen to stay in London and send
me away by myself. Only bad children are sent away, children
who are very naughty and can't live with their mommy because they are so bad she can't have them anywhere near her.
The thought began to take root. At that time I began to realize
I just had to start pleasing everybody or I would never survive.

Alone In A Strange Land

The table was laid with bread and butter and little pink
things on a plate. The woman asked me, "Are you hungry?"

"No," I said.

She said, "You had a long journey. You must eat something."

I didn't know what the little pink things were. I started to
eat them, and I had never tasted anything like it before and I
said, "What are these?"

"Shrimp."

Right in the middle of eating I got up, ran out and spat
them out of my mouth. I was terrified that I was going to be
sent to hell, because I was raised in an Orthodox Jewish
family and had never eaten anything that wasn't strictly kosher.
I thought God would come down and smite me. Even at six
years old I knew what I could and could not eat.

I wasn't even told that I wasn't with a family of my own
religion. What a transition that would have to be. I believe it
was shortly after this time that I began to question my faith
and religion, even this young. I couldn't understand why God
would send me away like this and make me do the things my
family had taught me never to do, such as eat things I was not
supposed to eat. I was so frightened. I felt I would have to
starve to death.

My hosts were angry and didn't understand. When they
found out I was Jewish, they were totally horrified. The people
in this tiny little village in Somerset had never really seen a
Jew, and I certainly didn't look the conventional Jewish type.

Later on that night, when the woman said I would have to take a bath and go to bed, my panic intensified. I realized I was going to be there, live there — and where was my mother and how long was this going to go on? If I had to go to bed that night and actually sleep in that room, then the game was up for me. I had never been consulted, never been told anything about this. Everything was settled without my having anything to say again.

On Sunday they dressed me in the one dress that I had and took me to a place called a chapel. People were singing all kinds of songs that I had never heard before about somebody called Jesus.

In adult life I have learned from Jesus and love him dearly according to his teachings. I have no religion, just a simple deep faith that my Higher Power loves me. But as a little girl, I had no idea who He was and why everybody was singing to Him and about Him. I had to go to Sunday school and I couldn't understand why the prayers were so very different. It seemed that everything I had ever known, anything that was familiar to me had been completely taken away and changed.

Within a week or so the word was around that "this one" was different. I can remember walking down the street and having some of the children come up to me, hold me and rub their fingers in my hair. I had no idea what they were doing. I thought this was maybe a Somerset greeting. What they were actually doing was looking for horns. They'd been told that all Jews had horns and a tail. Fortunately, I escaped from the indignity of their trying to discover whether I had a tail.

My feelings of aloneness, abandonment, terror and helplessness now began to grow at a rapid rate. I don't think I laughed for two years. Every day something seemed to happen to frighten me even more. I became a complete people-pleaser. I would do anything rather than incur anyone's wrath. If people were ever angry with me, I couldn't deal with it. Half the time I didn't know how to behave because I didn't know these people. I didn't understand their beliefs, I didn't understand the food they ate and I didn't know what on earth they were doing. Everything was a mystery to me and no one was there to solve that mystery for me.

On very rare occasions my mother or grandmother would telephone from London, and after I had spoken to them I would be silent for hours. I did cry a little then. I would always ask them, "When am I coming home? Let me come home. I want to be home. I want to be with you."

The answer was always, "You're better off there."

I met the other members of the family, including a married daughter I really liked. She was warm and loving and let me go to her house whenever I could. She only lived next door, but there was alienation from her sister and her mother because she had married beneath her and had six sons to prove how irresponsible she was.

About six months after I had come to Highbridge, two of her sons began to take a special interest in me. I was close to eight years old. They were considerably older. They began to touch and examine my body. Having come from being molested at home and having it happen again created unbelievable despair. I wasn't even among familiar people. I didn't tell anybody here in Somerset, for these people were even more emotionally unavailable to me than my own family.

When I cried sometimes at the news broadcasts on the radio or the telephone calls, they would say, "Oh, my goodness. Here we go again. Well, she just can't have any calls anymore or listen to the radio."

In order to try to compensate, my mother sent me a beautiful doll I called Queenie. The people I lived with allowed me to hold Queenie for one half hour every Sunday and that was all. I remember being in the house one day alone and managing to open the door where they locked her. I took her out and held her, and I was severely punished because the woman came home and found me holding her.

It's difficult to describe the pain of that particular time, the denial of any kind of love or healthy touching, the complete helplessness and the terror of not being able to share with anybody what I was going through because I didn't know how to put it into words. Even if there had been anybody there, I wouldn't have known how to say it. It was painful beyond words to me.

I was well cared for physically, well dressed and well fed, but my loneliness and ignorance of what was happening in London, not knowing after each air raid whether my family was alive or dead and not being told anything, caused a pain that became overwhelming. Shortly before my eighth birthday I made a decision that I really wanted to die. I set about doing just that. I stopped eating, wouldn't sleep, acted out in school, wouldn't talk to anybody and just withdrew entirely into myself. I didn't cry because I knew better. All I would say was, "I want to go home."

At about this time I had chicken pox, closely followed by the measles, and was very ill. Because I was so ill my grandmother came down to see me. I begged and pleaded with her to take me back. She would not do that. Even now, as a woman and a mother, I still cannot accept the fact that I was sent away for my own safety. I believe children's safety is with their parents if they love them, if they nourish them and nurture them. That's the way it would always be for me. This is simply my opinion, out of my own circumstances. It is not the same for everybody.

I must have eventually got through to my grandmother because, as my condition deteriorated, there were a lot of letters and telephone calls going back and forth. I was finally told that I was being sent back to London. Nobody came to get me for what seemed an eternity.

At this time I was eight years old. One day I was labeled again, put on the train in care of the guard, and sent back to London. My mother forgot to pick me up and I waited for hours in the station until the police constable saw me there. They contacted her because of the labels I had on me.

Home To The Blitz

The welcome home was less than cordial. I was a nuisance and had always been a nuisance since pregnancy. It was made very clear to me that, having got my way, I had better behave myself. So naturally I did everything I could to make sure I would not be sent away again. In the house I took care of my mother. I went to school. I was a good "little woman." And I was desperately unhappy. I was constantly afraid that one false move and I'd be back on the bus.

By this time in London the bombing had accelerated. There wasn't a night or a day when we didn't have several air raids. By this time daylight bombing had started, and there was a certain excitement to this because we never knew what was going to happen. As children, we didn't fully comprehend the danger, but we loved the unpredictability of sometimes missing school.

My mother refused to go to a bomb shelter. We used to go down into the cellar. I can remember a little dog I had who would begin to cry and whine and run under the table about 20 minutes before the planes came over. The bombs would come down silently and stop, then whistle down and explode. We never knew where they would land. However, the fear I had during these raids was nothing compared to the fear I had of being sent away again.

I was eventually sent away to Oxford for another year and it didn't matter how I begged not to go. I went.

In that year, which is almost a complete blank in my memory, I made myself very ill. I was so terribly unhappy and felt so lost that I didn't know how to do anything else. Becoming ill was the only way I got attention. All I knew was that what I wanted didn't count, that the Big People constantly lied when they said they cared about me. The knowledge that *I was not important* took root.

At the time this was going on, people were cold and distant with me. I can remember being in this house in Oxford, feeling deadly ill and being completely ignored — mainly, I assume, because they didn't know what to do with me.

The children of war suffer from post-traumatic stress disorder as much as its combat veterans. It's true, as shown in the film *Of Hope and Glory,* that some children had a great time and a lot of fun, but that wasn't my war. Possibly this was connected with the fact that I was sent away and brought back, sent away and brought back, so that I never had any continuous security. I never had any real knowledge of where I was going to be. The fear of being sent away again made me such a good girl. I suffered the indignities of a child who insisted on coming back. I heard that from my grandmother, my parents and my aunts and uncles.

I had to grow up very quickly. After I made myself ill in Oxford and came back, I had from somewhere the strength and aggressiveness to insist I would not go away again. This time *I would not go!*

What this experience left me with as an adult was that, no matter what, I would never, ever let my children go away from me or I would never put them away. They never went to summer camp. They never went to boarding school. I would have scrubbed floors or even prostituted myself rather than let those children go away from me. It was interesting to look at the kind of parent I became. I finally began to realize I was being too protective of my children, trying to overcompensate for the horror that I'd been through in my childhood. I had to learn to change my perfectionistic parenting. My son Colin went to camp once. Guess who suffered the most?

I was in London in the worst of the blitz, but that was better than being away. I remember the feelings of fear every time I heard bombs fall. They were very close.

I remember coming out of the house one morning, before my parents could stop me, to see that all the houses around me were razed except ours. I saw a dead person. I saw dead animals. The fire, the smoke and the stench were something I would never forget. I still have a hard time when I smell meat burning. Finally our house was bombed, too.

People say that children are too young to feel things — another "grown-up" lie. I tell people now that children do know. They do understand.

During the blitz my mother also took in refugees from Germany, Poland and Russia who had escaped from the concentration camps. People would congregate in my mother's home and talk about pain, grief and what was going on in the camps as if I weren't there. The result for me was a fear like that of a child who knows other children are being beaten by their own parents. There is always the fear that one day "it might happen to me, too."

The Way Out

Discovery of the "why" of my pain and fear took a lot of work with therapists, inpatient and outpatient treatment, and the loving support of the 12-Step Movement. Those of us who react tearfully to commercials of family bliss, and don't know why, are harboring the confusion of long ago. As a questioning small child we wondered, "Does it ever end?" The pain and anguish of "I must be bad" haunts us endlessly, until recognition of our right to be happy emerges through the fog. The "fog" represents our childhood that cannot be explained. The brutality and violation of children's rights are incomprehensible, and as adults we often overlook what happened to us as children. In coming to terms with the grief we experience, we have to think as a child until the feelings are resolved by acceptance and adjustment.

I can remember in my own treatment the frustration of trying to describe to therapist after therapist this "thing" that was inside me screaming to get out. When I saw the movie "Alien," I found the visual aid I had been seeking. Something slimy, horrible, ravenous and terrifying was in there poisoning my life. When I saw that, anguish and relief held hands. Delayed stress came flooding in.

The following chapters will identify recognition, treatment and recovery. Please take time to read and respond to the questions that appear at the close of each chapter. Keep a journal of your responses and/or reactions.

Begin with these questions before you read on.

1. What is the primary feeling that surfaces when you think of your childhood? Let the feeling flow and write whatever comes without rationalizing.
2. How do you think your family saw you? Hero, rotten kid, cutesy, lovable, silent, withdrawn, etc. Describe in detail.
3. What wasn't fair?
4. Define "normal" as you understand it.

3

 Stages Of
Grief

When I was a child, I thought as a child. When I was grown, I still thought as a child.

At the age of 31, seven months pregnant, I stood at my mother's coffin and cried. Within minutes one of my aunts was by my side, telling me urgently to stop crying. "You'll hurt the baby."

I stopped immediately, automatically, without question, and did not cry for myself or for the death of my mother for another 10 years. Nor did I cry for her life or mine.

Yvonne Kaye

Grief is the final expression of love.

Lorna Helsinger

The stages of grieving are important in terms of recovery. Only when grief is accepted by the Mourner can the healing begin.

In the case of the Adult Child Mourner, it is essential to recognize that there is, in fact, grief. The first stage, *denial,* is so insidious in its subtlety that grieving often comes as a surprise. People recognize sadness, anger and sometimes tears on certain occasions. They rarely see those reactions as grieving, but rather as emotions that need to be controlled.

These levels of grieving may not always be experienced in the order I have them written. Much of the pattern is already established in the survival skills learned in the formative years. For example, if a person reacts angrily to most situations, anger will be the first indication of grief. Sometimes a person will shut down right away. That is denial.

Regardless of the impact, people will grieve the way they live their lives on a day-to-day basis. At whatever stage the grieving begins, the other levels will be experienced at some time according to the speed of awareness entering the Mourner's psyche.

Let's discuss the levels individually. While you are reading, have pen and paper ready to write down *anything* that enters your mind. Do not let your brain "argue" you out of whatever comes to you. The brain is the great rationalizer. To get in touch with feelings, let your brain take a nap.

This is one of the tools to remove the blocks. Remember, your attitude toward pain and grief today is a direct result of your childhood trauma. Remember, too, that each person's experience is unique to that person. Institute the philosophy now: "You can only compare yourself to yourself."

Denial And Isolation

Small children do not verbalize, they internalize.

Yvonne Kaye

Whatever children have to do to survive, they will do. Most of their survival skills are developed at a subconscious level, without either the knowledge or permission of the child. There is a natural tendency to pretend that nothing wrong is happening and that the family and its behavior are perfectly normal. Those two words "perfectly normal" are engraved on the subconscious of grieving children from dysfunctional families. A great deal of shame is attached to those words because the child has no frame of reference as to what is or is not normal. As the confusion and discomfort are so prevalent, all the child wants is for "it" to go away. When "it" doesn't, there is an assumption that the child must have been bad. The striving for perfection usually starts here.

Denial: "Nothing is working here, so I'll pretend it isn't happening."

Isolation: "If I tell my friends at school I'm busy with my family at home, I won't have to join in any after-school activities or go to their homes."

Denial is insidious. It is uncontrollable. Emotional shutdown is common for children seeking the love and support that just are not there. Being children equals being total victims. They cannot pack their bags and leave home at the age of six, so they vacate the premises emotionally. Even though the environment and the Big People in it create feelings of pain and fear, small children pretend that all is well at home.

In the movie *"Soft is the Heart of a Child,"* little Lisa tells the school counselor, "My mommy and daddy are taking us to Disney World. They made a birthday party for me. And my grandma and grandpa came. All my friends were there, too, and we had a lot of fun. Then my mommy and daddy went out to dinner on their own . . ."

She trails into silence. The counselor then responds, oh so very gently, "That's how you would like it to be, isn't it, Lisa?" Lisa is into denial because her young life has become unmanageable. She lives in an alcoholic household with her doll, upon whom she showers all her love. There are only pain and fantasy for Lisa.

Small children have no control over family situations and the Big People who create them. They have no say in anything that happens because they are helpless — but they don't know that. They feel responsible. They try to mend the lives of their dysfunctional parents, watching from their foxholes the behaviors of their siblings. They observe the craziness of others who do not know how to cope with all of this either. They go further into denial and frequently into isolation.

For these children, "stable" is a place where horses live, not a state of mind. They have no concept of peacefulness, love and communication. They feel nothing that is recognizable to them. As adults in recovery, we know that the emotions are there, but that the fear of expressing them is so strong, it acts as an anesthetic.

Another form of denial is the perennially cheerful, smiling child. Everything is "fine," "great" and "wonderful." Marilyn was such a child. Her smiles took her into adult life through drugs, alcohol and horrendous relationships. She was always "the life of the party," smiling, giggling loudly and shrilly, laughing at everyone's jokes whether they were funny or not.

Marilyn's family was severely dysfunctional. Both parents were alcoholic, as were four of her brothers and two sisters. Two of her brothers were in and out of prison consistently, and the family secrets were many. *But nobody talked about anything because everything was okay!* Marilyn had a "fantastic" childhood, mainly because she was never asked to define the word. Her drugs of choice were alcohol, speed and love. This laughing, highly energized, "let's-have-a-ball" woman suffered with colitis, ulcers and intestinal problems until she entered treatment. The behavior continued into her middle 20s, when her younger sister was killed and Marilyn stopped laughing. Sometimes it takes a major tragedy to come out of denial. Ironic, isn't it? One tragedy puts us in and another takes us out.

The message that both little Lisa and Marilyn gave to themselves was "peace at any price." Hiding for one and entertaining for the other became behaviors that were part of their survival plan.

It has been established that small children make very powerful decisions, usually damaging ones, in order to survive. Even though they are not consciously aware of the need, they yearn for the warm loving arms of their parents, for total and unconditional love. They long to be held, stroked, kissed, cuddled and told, "You are a miracle." They look for healthy direction, answers, truth. They ache for the basic human rights that any child needs. They long to be children.

When they don't get their needs met, they panic and act in whatever way soothes their pain of rejection and abandonment. Denial and isolation are the tools of the class clown, the angry child, the depressed child. All receive negative attention, but negative attention is better than none. Keeping the peace is essential. Being seen and not heard is a requirement. Shutting down, not feeling and not loving, will keep the child safe. If the child hides in its room, it feels secure — until one of those Big People tells them it's not natural to be away from the family. What a message: "Go away; come closer."

What a difference it would make if one of these injured children would know what questions to ask. So often the children are too intimidated to even think the questions, let alone ask them. Whether a child is raised in a dysfunction of alcohol, mental illness, a dying sibling, pathological cleanliness or other neuroses, the message is the same. "You had better learn to fend for yourself. Grow up — act your age. You can't trust anyone."

Picture the Only Child. Not only do they suffer the same indignities as children with siblings, they take total responsibility in all areas of the dysfunction. Children from dysfunctional families have been defined as taking on the roles of Hero, Scapegoat, Lost Child and Mascot. The only child is all four and has no support from siblings. They are an angle in the triangle

of family dysfunction and their grief is brutal, as their position
in the triangle moves according to the moods and whims of the
Big People concerned. Whatever skills they acquire to survive
are exacerbated by the loneliness. There are no siblings to
whom they can turn to share their history, none with whom
they can validate their sanity. Did it happen? Really happen?

All Adult Child Mourners have immense problems with
control and intimacy — Only Children have incredible odds
to face in those areas. Because of their triangle involvement,
Only Children who are Adult Child Mourners are demandingly
passive/aggressive as a rule. They need, demand and expect
attention, positive or negative, as long as it is attention. The
level of perfectionism is almost crippling. They have to be the
best, have the best, be the most important and nothing is ever
good enough. In most cases Only Children are bottomless
pits when it comes to emotional need.

Being an Only Child and then a parent of four, I remember
being appalled when my children would argue and fight.
"You should love one another," I would wail, before I knew
this was a perfectionism attack. My children, in turn, would
look at me in amazement while waiting for the people in
white coats to take me away.

Sometimes Only Children are lucky in having some
members of the extended family to help out. For the most
part, their denial is impenetrable.

The basis of denial is unawareness. It is often not a case of
looking at a situation and telling oneself, "I don't want to deal
with this." It's simply, "I don't know."

A positive aspect of denial is that in some ways it protects
children from feeling what is unchangeable in their environment. Our social service agencies are simply not equipped to
deal with the millions of children who are currently living in
painful households. The family courts have much to learn in
dealing with incested children, visitations with abusive parents, absentee parents and other abusive situations. Mercifully,
children in these families shut down because in reality they
have to stay where they are. There's nowhere else to go.

As I am writing this part of denial, memories are flooding
into my mind. That's how long some of this takes. It further

reinforces my belief that the Higher Power will only deliver what we can deal with when the time is right. I know that a lot of the therapy I have undergone in the last 15 years or so is responsible now for the awareness I have. I could not have handled it then. Patience is something we need to cultivate. We have learned to be patient with others. Here's the *big one*. We have to be patient with our own growth and changes. This is very new to us.

How many of you, on reading this, remember how the Big People became silent when you entered a room? What did you think and feel at that time? Take a break from this and write down as clearly as you can the feelings you recall on any given situation of "sudden silence."

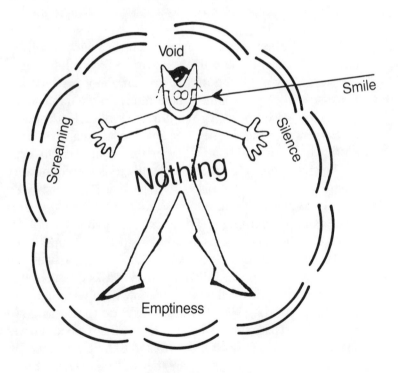

Figure 3.1. The Isolated Child

Recognition

From my experience, I disagree with people who say that
96 percent of all families in the United States are dysfunctional. Possibly the majority of families have a dysfunction
of some kind. But it largely depends on the definition of
dysfunction. Mine is: *Dysfunction* is any situation in which
a child is denied its basic healthy human survival rights: to
be held, kissed, cuddled, told it's a miracle and made to feel
secure in commonsense direction from healthy parents.

Figure 3.2 has caused many people to start thinking that
possibly their adult behavior was a result of being robbed of
their childhood.

This figure signifies the environment in which a child is
raised. The outer circle is the boundary over which they cannot step. They are living normally in an abnormal situation.
Because of their environment, children are often traumatized
when they leave home to go to nursery school, kindergarten
or elementary school. They quickly discover that they don't
know what "normal" is, and they are thrown into confusion.

The child begins to recognize that there is something very
different in the "school place." "There is a Big Person who
listens and plays without getting so rough that they hurt. This
place is clean and bright. They have real parties at holiday
times. The Big Person helps if a child is stuck. Sometimes other
Big People come and talk. Someone called 'Nurse' makes you
feel better, and someone called 'Counselor' asks questions that
make you think she really wants to know what you think. But
something is wrong here. Other kids ask you to play or go to
their homes. That's scary. I feel different to them. I could never
take anyone home. I don't know what to expect. I'm afraid."

In their fear, children erect another wall — a layer of protection. They begin to feel there's something outside of their
boundary that frightens them because it is different. The closer
the teacher or the other children get, the stronger the defense.
They begin to question:

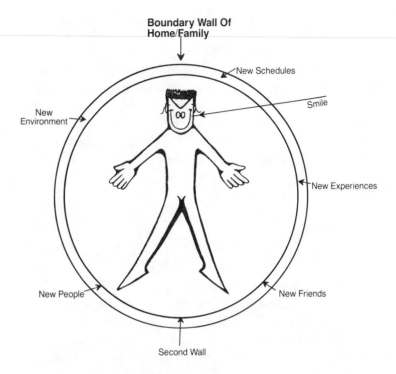

Figure 3.2. Boundaries

- "How come other kids play without being hurting?"
- "Why is this Big Person so nice?"
- "If I make a mistake, will I be beaten?"
- "I'm not going to trust any of this." (Subconscious thought.)
- "If I go to Billy's house, will his mom be screaming as soon as we get there? I'm not going."
- "If I go to Jenny's party, will it really be a party or a fight?"
- "It's different for me — I'll stay out of all this. It's safer."
- "Why would any of these kids want to be my friend? People aren't like this at home, so I must be a bad kid at home."
- "Nobody loves me. My mom and dad tell me I'm a nuisance, so why would anyone want me to go to their house?"
- "Not me!"

Children start to compare at this stage. If they do create enough courage to venture into a normal family home, the realization that they are "different" won't be long in coming.

The realization that *something is wrong* is the beginning of a breakthrough of denial. Some children stay in denial until they become adults. The pain of their helplessness is too much to bear, so they retreat into oblivion once more.

Learning to trust a Big Person is a difficult step for a child to take. The knowledge that there is such a thing as feeling safe in one's family, while knowing that safety doesn't exist in their family, is shattering.

Ambivalence

- "If only I could have been better, prettier, brighter or had better grades, they'd care for me."
- "If only I could make them love one another, I know they could love me."
- "If only I hadn't been born, they would be fine."
- "If it isn't the same here as it is at Billy's house, it must be my fault."
- "I know I can do something to change all this."

There are two basic attitudes in grieving what was not. One is healthier than the other. Even though children have a limited frame of reference, they know that the behavior of dysfunctional parents is not quite right. One child will think, "What did I do wrong?" Another child may think in a healthier way, "What's the matter with these crazy grown-ups?" Both these attitudes are carried into adult life.

Barry was a child of two workaholic parents. He had to work with them in their restaurant from a very young age. There was never any recognition of his involvement, only beatings if he was not up to par. If he forgot an order, dropped a dish, asked for some money or committed any other offense, he would receive a reaction of martyrdom from his father and a slap from his mother. Barry became an overachiever in every way, including placating people to have them love him.

Being highly intelligent, he tried to please by doing school work for other students. He was never included in their social activities or friendships in return. He thought that ingratitude was normal, even to the point of being told that he wasn't invited to the events because they knew he wouldn't be comfortable.

He accepted all of this as perfectly normal. As he grew older he realized that even if he had been invited, he would not have known how to behave. His only messages were, "It is better to give than to receive" and "If you don't do it well or fast enough, then you are inadequate."

Barry grew into a man who felt inadequate in every area — business, relationships, family and creativity. He bought the whole package. Abused children frequently do because they have nothing to which they can compare. When Barry did something for a person who thanked him or complimented him, he became lost in the *Imposter Syndrome.*

One of the areas of grieving the childhood that never was is believing that one is an imposter. If there are good feelings one day, they won't last because I don't deserve them. The most violent of all reactions is, "If you knew what I was *really* like, you wouldn't be so complimentary!"

These people almost drown in self-analysis. They look inward until they get caught up in their own intestines. They are forever looking for character defects and overindulging in shame and blame. This is a mechanism to create a perfect person whom *someone will love!*

Not so for Christine, who as a child learned the healthier attitude. The Imposter Syndrome for her is the other person. She knows she is real and regards her ups and downs as normal everyday living. She indulges in a few "if onlys," but then focuses on herself to rid her mind of trying to change what was and get what she never had.

Christine is not totally healthy (Who is?), but she is infinitely healthier than Barry, who constantly beats on himself. She sees her parents — whose background and behavior were identical to those of Barry's parents — as sick, frightened people whose only sources of identity were possessions and money in the bank.

Some human behavior scientists, researchers I respect highly, will tell you the fundamental difference between Barry and Christine. I can't. As there are different energies, so there are different personalities, and some *get it* quicker than others. I believe I was a combination of Barry and Christine — it just took me longer.

When I was sent away from home at age six to "be safe" during the war without a word of explanation, I instantly became inadequate in my own mind and decided I was bad. Not once did I think there was anything wrong with my parents. My frame of reference and my behavior were based on what had been fed to me from Big People. I did nothing, reacted as "normal" by doing as I was told, like a little robot. At that time I certainly felt alien to my surroundings.

Up to this time I had been raised mostly by my grandparents as the only natural child of my dysfunctional parents. I thought during my childhood that this erratic, crazy, violently angry man who married my mother was my father. It wasn't until my 21st birthday that I was told, by letter from my father while we were living in the same house, that my mother had been pregnant with me by another man. In my child's mind I knew there was something very wrong with that marriage. He would call her a whore and tell her to get back on the streets where she belonged. I could never understand why he said that, but I knew instinctively it was my fault. So I did what most children in screwed-up families do to survive. I did what I was told, always, without question.

Living in another home with other strange people, my feelings began to rise up just a little. Sometimes I felt good, sometimes bad. When bad things happened to me, I knew that was right. After all, if I had been a good child I wouldn't have been sent away. To make it worse, after she sent me away, my mother took in foster children. I simply couldn't grasp that. It was illogical. I was a foster child, and I had a real mother who took in foster children. I spent a great deal of time trying to see how I could get my mother to love me enough to take me home.

"After all," I reasoned, "good children stay with their parents."

A great deal of damage is done to children in the conspiracy of silence. It builds up walls. I believe noncommunication is worse than negative messages. Again, noncommunication is looking at a situation that is nonexistent. In the same category of grieving something that "never was," it is just as frustrating.

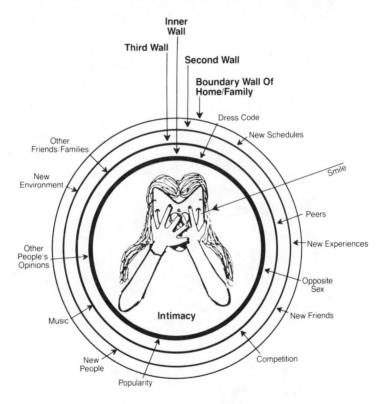

Figure 3.3. Noncommunication

As each stage of growth occurs, the walls build up. They are constructed largely of passive/aggressive patterns. For example, saying it's okay when it isn't, just to keep people at bay. In the center, the child is living in its chronological growth, its definition of intimacy. The closer a person gets to them, the thicker the walls of protection.

Some of these fears have been related to me by patients who recognized their dilemmas from this small chart. They say this ambivalence caused a malfunctioning in every aspect of their lives, raising questions such as:

- "Why can't I have a good friendship?"
- "Why am I so jealous of my friend who has other friends?"
- "Why am I so threatened when I have to meet new people?"

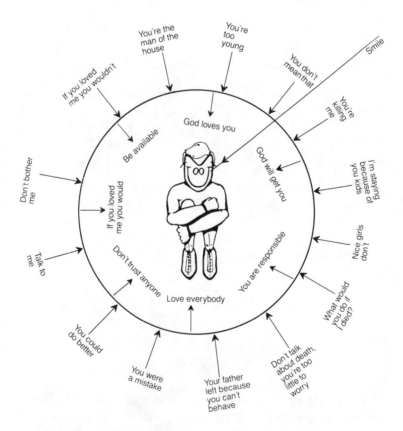

Figure 3.4. Confusion Of The Adult Child Mourner

Elizabeth told me that when these questions arise she usually does her invisible disappearing act. Suddenly she needs "time to think" and goes away for a couple of days or is incommunicado. Of course, the last thing she does is think sufficiently clearly to bring some resolution to these questions. Instead, she simply hides away until she can start the agonizing self-analysis all over again. I was told many years ago, when I first began to listen, that if I counseled myself, I had a fool for a counselor. We cannot do this alone.

The ambivalence of the Adult Child Mourner stems from not understanding emotions. Being rigid in an attempt to gain security (If I never change, everything will be fine), Mourners are frightened of the emotional roller coaster that assails them. Feelings change from good to bad so quickly at times that they cancel each other out. The result? Numbness or confusion. As confusion comes before clarity, it's infinitely preferable to "nothingness."

Many Adult Child Mourners have suffered the feeling of invisibility, which sounds like a misnomer. It is not — it is further evidence that in childhood the dysfunctional messages stick. The majority of people in this world today would react in the same way if they met ten people, nine liked them and one didn't. Where would the emphasis be? Right — on the one who did not like them. The rationalizing goes from a dishonest, "Who gives a darn anyway?" to, "I'm not worth liking." In between we have, "I wonder why? The others like me; why doesn't she?"

Years ago when I began my own journey of recovery, a therapist told me to take a good look around me to see how much I was loved — to stop taking people close to me for granted. Her actual statement was, "Your kids don't care what you look like in the morning. They accept you, regardless."

Those of us in the human services field suffer severely from the Imposter Syndrome. "Helping" people can lead to a self-assessment that usually goes like this: "If they *really* knew what I was like . . ."

At this point, I'd like to recommend the first book I ever read on the subject. It helped me so much that I recommend it often.

Why Am I Afraid To Tell You Who I Am? by John Powell, S.J., is a joy. The entire title is: *Why Am I Afraid To Tell You Who I Am? Because If I Do And You Don't Like Me, That's All I've Got.* It explained so much to me about a different kind of grieving — self-esteem. I learned that one of the reasons I got stuck was my fear of the next level.

Anger And Rage

Anger is healthy. Rage is the result of anger that is not expressed. People have enormous difficulties in recognizing anger, mainly because . . .

1. It was never allowed in their dysfunctional family.
2. There was too much of it in the family.
3. It is a societal no-no.

There is confusion, even in the 12-Step Programs, with regard to this particular emotion. It is said that there is no such thing as justifiable anger, that it is a question of power. I do not agree.

Viktor Frankl, in his incredible book *Man's Search For Meaning*, discusses the idea that people make conscious decisions about the way they feel. This amazing man wrote that statement while incarcerated in Auschwitz Concentration Camp. It made an enormous impact on me when I read it. At the time I was almost drowning in the toilet bowl of self-pity, wanting to die and at the same time screaming, "Don't flush!"

If people make conscious decisions to be angry at what has been perpetrated against them in their innocent childhood, I believe they have to do so in order to let it go. If these feelings of anger are suppressed, the result is either rage or denial. In addition to making conscious decisions as to the way they feel, I believe people decide how long to feel it before they recognize that they are continuing the problem and have to release.

Anger is a powerfully positive emotion if channeled constructively. If it is ignored and denied, the rage takes over and the control leaves. There are many components to anger, some of which are . .

a. Frustration   e. Blame
b. Sarcasm   f. Guilt
c. Shame   g. Vengeance
d. Hurt   h. Primal Emotion

If you refer to Figure 3.3, you will note that the inner circle close to the child is thick and heavy. This is destructive anger — another way to keep people away. Anyone who gets close to that fortress of intimacy is demolished. I mentioned earlier that Mourners exhibit passive/aggressive behavior. They can lull people into a sense of false security by appearing to be friendly until *the boundary is crossed.* Then the anger and aggressiveness take over.

This aspect of the grieving process is difficult to comprehend or explain. There is a definite push/pull behavior as the Adult Child Mourner gets close to a situation they have longed for. Why, then, the closing up, the retreat to the emotional prison? They want it — they don't! Come here — go away!

Again, consider the frame of reference these children had in their formative years. The dysfunctional parents kept saying, not necessarily in words, "Go away, come closer." In their own sickness, they wanted to have the child as something to love but also were afraid of the responsibility of loving.

How far do we go back to find their childhood grief, their parents' childhood? This is not safe. It is not productive thinking for recovery. We hear about blame and shame. Many books have been written on the subject. I feel that blaming and shame are both part of the recovery process, natural reactions to the unknown joys of the childhood that could have been. Without owning these feelings, recovery comes to a standstill.

Again, to refer to Frankl, we make conscious decisions but we don't have to hold on to them. They are part of the process of recovery.

Rage is explosive. It is dangerous and needs to be defused. Recognition and acceptance of anger as a healthy emotion can be the "bomb squad" to remove that detonator. At first when realizations occur, the Mourner feels violated; after all, we are talking first-degree theft here! A whole childhood has been stolen.

The effects of the robbery can last a lifetime in terms of seeking the love that never was. Adult Child Mourners, in their quest for love, will seek out that which is familiar — unavailable people. They will find significant others and co-workers to rescue and take care of, only to discover that when they need help, no one is there. The next ingredient of rage is *resentment*.

Mourners in the grip of resentment can retreat into martyrdom, plan vengeance, pick up an addiction or become involved in yet another unrewarding relationship to compare just how bad it was with the way it still is. Rage is responsible for self-mutilation, emotional illness and some physical conditions, such as ulcers, colitis, heart problems, high blood pressure and acceleration of some cancers. So what exactly is it?

Rage is a condition of destructive anger that gets out of control to the point that Mourners create an environment of self-fear. They believe that if they begin to express their rage, they never will be able to stop. Or they believe they will die. This second reason is usually a childhood power decision made when the pain was too unbearable. It is also a form of denial and ambivalence. The bottom line is fear.

"If I express what I'm truly feeling, no one will like me. What if I do say it, and then they say they don't know what I'm talking about! They'll be so mad they won't talk to me again."

Let me state clearly here, having had to deal with my own rage, that sooner or later it is taken out of the Mourner's hands.

The last aspect of rage is the feeling of stupidity. "I felt like such a fool getting into another abusive relationship." Couple that with the confusion of not knowing anything *but* an abusive pattern, and the terror mounts.

So here we have the wonderful trio of crazies:

> Violation
> Resentment
> Stupidity

Formidable, aren't they?

Craziness and guilt pervade this entire stage of grief. Thoughts battle inside the Mourner's head: "I must be crazy to stay in this family/relationship/job. I must stay in this family/relationship/job to make it better."

The bad crazies come with our rage at not knowing, not understanding *why we do what we do.*

The guilt accompanies our feeling responsible; that it's our fault; that we don't understand *why we do what we do.*

Most people know what guilt is. Normally it is used as a weapon to make people do what you want them to do. Parents use it a great deal, as do spouses and lovers. Friends use it rarely because friendship is the highest form of love. My definition of guilt is simple. I merely replace the word "guilt" with the word "power." In that way I can decide whether I am feeling a power greater than my own or whether I am trying to change something or someone, which is impossible. The powerful impact of the serenity prayer and its simple, beautiful, logical message is a force in my life today:

"God grant me the serenity to accept the things I cannot change, courage to change the things I can, *and wisdom to know the difference.*"

Adult Child Mourners fume at the humiliation they suffered and wonder why they either humiliate others in order to feel good or let people walk all over them. Self-inflicted punishment is the order of the day. It feels right because that was always the way it was. The Adult Child Mourner does not see, at this stage of grieving, that there are other options.

Rage is a killer that has been responsible for many emotional and physical deaths. It is an out-of-control condition. Because of the strong place it holds in the lives of Adult Child Mourners, it is essential that counselors, psychologists, psychiatrists and all involved in the human services field comprehend its magnitude and its permanently destructive capabilities.

Adjustment

Most literature dealing with grief uses the word "acceptance." The only use I have for it is to help in recognizing that there was and is a problem and a need to grieve the childhood that never was — and that's all. If the word acceptance is used in the levels of grieving, it seems to me that there has to be an entire condoning and forgiving. Grieving and forgiving are two mutually exlusive conditions, and acceptance is not relevant here. Time will address that — it isn't an immediate resolution.

As life is a series of adjustments, whether normal or dysfunctional, the word *adjustment* is infinitely more palatable to me. There is no rigid code in adjustment. The very word means *change* — another nasty one. There is no penalty in adjustments. They present themselves when the time is right, when the lesson has been learned.

When Adult Child Mourners recognize the conditions of childhood, they frequently want to make it all better at once. "Okay, so I know what a lousy life I led and know how rotten my parents were. That's fine. I'm all right now — it explains everything!"

Back to the drawing board — *denial.*

The person making such a statement will find sooner or later that life has not changed. Immediate acceptance is simply not feasible. The Adult Child Mourner needs to realize that, as long as it took to get to that information, it's going to take a while to resolve and recover.

Television commercials have taught children all about immediate gratification. From instant potatoes to getting a loan for whatever is required, this message is implanted in the child's mind. The information is, "I want it and I want it now because I never had it!"

I recall going to a conference once with a friend. It was geared toward Adult Children of Dysfunctional Families. We both felt that the vast majority of the participants were the rudest, pushiest, most unpleasant people we had ever met. We were used to workshops and conferences with recovering addicted people who wanted to make amends and who "did guilt" very well. Suddenly here were all these "It's My Turn" T-shirts, covering ample, thrusting bosoms and chests, just daring us to get in their way. The buffet supper was a joke. Any adult child, as we both are, could see that mealtimes must have been nightmares for most of these people. I spent a great many years of my life working with motorcycle gangs, and I was much more careful with these Adult Children than the tattooed, cursing gang members I encountered.

That weekend was sad. What was useful for me was that I saw how far I had come in knowing that treatment is a gift, not a punishment; that recovery was there and I took it, but no one had to be destroyed so I could get well. I know now that we all have choices, and many times they are difficult to make because we are used to only two: fight or flight.

Part of adjustment is an acceptance of sorts. As it says so magnificently on Page 449 in the *Big Book* of Alcoholics Anonymous:

Acceptance is the answer to all my problems today. When I am disturbed, it is because I find some person, place, thing or situation — some fact of my life — unacceptable to me, and I can find no serenity until I accept that person, place, thing or situation as being exactly the way it is supposed to be at this moment. Nothing, absolutely nothing happens in God's world by mistake. Until I could accept my alcoholism, I could not stay sober; unless I accept life completely on life's terms, I cannot be happy. I need to concentrate not so much on what needs to be changed in the world as on what needs to be changed in me and in my attitudes.

Shakespeare said, 'All the world's a stage, and all the men and women merely players': He forgot to mention that I was the chief critic.

It seems like a dichotomy. Acceptance of what has to be done is essential. Acceptance that it had to happen and that it was a child's responsibility is not.

I feel moved to make a statement here. I have heard people say, "There is no such thing as a total victim." Rot! They refer to the "seductive child." These two premises are largely responsible for children not getting the help to which they have a right.

A child is a total victim.

Little Jenny was orally raped from the age of approximately one year. She recalls being tied in a chair with her hands behind her back while her father thrust his penis into her mouth — she was three. Was she seductive? Was she at fault? Was she not a total victim? This went on for nine years — what do you think?

Jenny has had to accept a lot of situations.

1. That her father will never admit or apologize.
2. That her recovery is in her hands.
3. That she doesn't have to be the perfect daughter just because he no longer abuses her.
4. That as a married woman with children of her own, she does not have to overcompensate.
5. That she can break the cycle of whatever brutalities her parents experienced in their own growing up.
6. That she does not have to feel shame or guilt over what happened to her when she was little.
7. That she can say no.
8. That she can change her attitudes and choose the people, places and things in her life that support and care for her.
9. That she has a right to treatment.

Sophie was a child in conflict, abandoned and rejected. That conflict remained in her entire life until recently, coming from within herself. She told me:

What did I do to retain relationships? Well, anything — anything rather than to allow anybody to leave me. Separation anxiety was a constant part of my life and it didn't matter who was leaving. Just that they were leaving. Or if I had to go away and they didn't, I was being sent away. In the few relationships I've had with men, most of them have been relatively long term, not because of the love and desire to stay together but rather that I was too afraid to let them go.

Sophie suffered a lot of emotional abuse as a result of that fear. The child who is raised in the kind of conflict she endured — that is a life-and-death situation every day — develops a tenacity that is devastating on an emotional level. Sophie just didn't recognize when relationships were over. She did not want to know things had become so bad, that the person just couldn't tolerate being with her. Because of the neglect in her childhood, she was extremely demanding of anybody in her life. "Taking hostages" was an understatement for her at that time. She just needed, needed, needed to have somebody there who would tell her she was the greatest, the best in every way. Nobody did, of course. She always selected somebody emotionally unavailable to her and who had other women in his life. That was to feed the need for the punishment Sophie had as a child, when she felt she didn't deserve anything good. If anything positive came to her, it wouldn't last because she had done something wrong and didn't deserve it.

In most friendships or family relationships that Adult Children Mourners had in growing up, when anything went wrong they *always* assumed the complete blame. Until quite recently, for example, I would listen and react to any negative opinion of me from people close to me, always believing it was my fault. This is what happens when children are born into chaos, born into instability, born to people who are frightened and insecure with no balance of their own.

I remember no happiness after the age of two. There were only fleeting moments of craziness that would appear to be happiness. To me one of the definitions of happiness is a sense of emotional security. It is knowing that those who love you are the same whether you are together or apart. That love doesn't end when you are away for the day. I always seemed to be with people, men especially, who could never give me the satisfaction of knowing who I was in their life. Or sometimes they did let me know, and I didn't want to accept that. So my fantasy would run riot. Then I would pretend I was the most important person to them and nobody else really mattered in the same way. I knew they were involved with a lot of other women and I really knew my wish-fantasy wasn't true. The pain was exactly the same pain I experienced on being sent away as a child. Sometimes I shared that story with the men in my life who were untreated and emotionally unavailable themselves. Then one of the things they would do when they could not control me was send me away, saying that it just couldn't work. Within a week they would be on the phone saying how much they missed me, and I would go right back.

In order to complete a healthy adjustment in the grieving process, the Adult Child Mourner has to confront necessary attitudinal changes. As the ultimate desire is to be able to let go of the past, these attitudinal changes have to be discussed in terms of what they could be. It is important to assess the level of self-confidence and self-esteem at this point. Doing this with a questionnaire is simplest.

Enter all this in your journal:

1. Create your own boundary circle. Put yourself in the middle and write in all the messages you can recall in your childhood. Give yourself time to do this — weeks, if necessary. It will take time.

2. Answer the questionnaire.

Relationship Questionnaire

1. What is the construction of your family of origin?
2. Where are you in your sibling hierarchy? (If you are an only child, consider your place in the extended family of cousins.)
3. Who was the most intelligent in your family?
4. Who was the most attractive?
5. Did you enjoy family visits/parties/picnics? If so, how? If not, why?
6. Were you comfortable with your schoolmates? If so, why? If not, why?
7. Who was the most popular person you knew in school? Describe this person and your feelings about him or her.
8. How important is it to you how people think of you?
9. Make a list of the key people in your life (whose opinions really matter).
10. What makes these people special?
11. How many people on your list (relatives, friends, colleagues) are there because they "should" be?

12. Were you on your own list? If not, write the reason why you were out. If you were, your self-confidence is pretty good!

With all these different people knocking over the boundaries that were set by the childhood family of origin, there can be a tendency to freeze assets. What this means is that fear overrides the desire and shuts down whatever emotions have become available in certain growth areas due to treatment or 12-Step Programs. Rock performer Sting sings of "the fortress around your heart." That aptly describes the Adult Child Mourner at this stage of grieving. Attitudinal changes are the direct result of ascertaining the right amount of adjustment that can be made safely and constructively. Adult Child Mourners will rarely let anyone in without building another wall, so they have to come to the decision that they will come out instead.

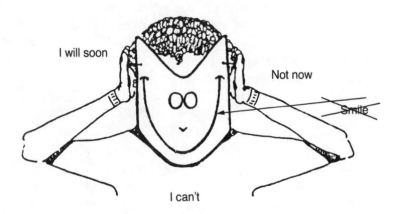

I will soon

Not now

Smile

I can't

Figure 3.5. Take Off The Mask

At this point, sabotage rears its ugly head. Because of the dysfunction of childhood there is very little trust regarding good feelings. The Adult Child Mourner cannot grasp that it is normal to sometimes feel good and sometimes feel bad. When they begin to feel good, the terror that they may lose it is a self-fulfilling prophecy. They recall that every time something good happened, it was followed by something bad. For example, a birthday party ended in a fight. Children associate these events as normal behavior — "that's life." As adults, this association creates sabotage. There is a deep-set negativity which precludes long-term joy. It is a partially subconscious attitudinal reaction. We are what we think, so statements such as the following are serious blocks to recovery:

"I feel great — something's bound to happen. This can't last."

"It's too good to be true."

Sabotage in adult life is self-inflicted. Viktor Frankl discusses this further in *Man's Search For Meaning.*

Look at Figure 3.5 again. Adult Child Mourners will take tiny steps at first — testing, testing, testing. They are so scared that the thought of risk is terrifying. Their concept of "healthy" is very distorted. Someone agreeing to disagree with something they said is World War III to them, so they often settle back into their self-made wombs until their resources gather strength and they try it again. Adult Child Mourners tend to believe that healthy love means total agreement on every issue. They have to learn that the freedom to agree to disagree is a prerequisite. There is still a tendency to believe that it's healthy for them to control every situation and everybody in it.

There are many attitudinal adjustments to be made after we recognize the myths of a happy childhood and a tower of painful, yet healthy reality sets in. Our attitude toward illness is an example.

I awoke in the night, sweating. As I lay in bed, my thoughts raced: "What's going on? Am I dying? Better just stay here quietly — nobody likes a sicko!" Hot flash after hot flash came and went. I didn't know what to do. Was this normal? I carefully pushed back the covers to relieve the heat and in a short time was freezing so I pulled them back on again, only to throw them off seconds later. I thought, "You should have listened to the doctor; there's no need to suffer like this."

I considered this, launching into an argument with myself regarding the *weakness* of women my age who couldn't hack it. I asked myself again — what was going on? This wasn't just a menopausal attack. Every part of my body ached. I wanted to get up, go downstairs and make a cup of tea, but it was

3:30 in the morning and I should be sleeping. Suppose I disturbed the rest of the household?

At this point I realized that all my childhood issues were flooding in. What did I really want to do? Get up and write. But this was in the middle of the night. To do something "unusual" like getting up in the middle of the night had been totally unacceptable in my crazy family of origin. To be unwell, frightened, restless or sleepless was not tolerated. In addition, it was a sinful waste of electricity to get up in the darkness. To be sick was such a nuisance to everybody — simply another attention-getter.

I used sickness a lot as a child. It was one way of getting attention, negative though it was. When that didn't work, I'd pretend to faint.

In retrospect I understand I was picking up on my mother's brand of behavior. If she was sick, in addition to being pathologically nice, no one could confront her. I realized that the insecure person can use illness as a crutch — I suppose the phrase "enjoying ill health" came from someone who understood it long before I did. It seems ironic to me that in my dysfunctional family only the "normal," the "conventional," was tolerated. It simply did not do to be up in the middle of the night, to be afraid of anything, to express any emotions. It had to be normal — that was the control. What was childhood anyway?

Peggy tells her childhood fear: darkness. She would hear her parents screaming and fighting. In her terror she would cry out, begging to have the light on, because the demons would be there to take her away. She knew she was responsible for her parents' marriage. She knew they would have been better together if she had never been born. She felt so responsible.

"I used to huddle in my bed, shaking and just wanting the noise to stop. I felt so helpless — I didn't know what to do. My legs were too weak for me to get out of bed, and if I had, all the things in the darkness of my room would have got me — so I just lay there and screamed."

Usually her father would come in and holler at her to shut up. She would plead to have the light on in the room, but he told her to grow up. (She was six when this started.) By begging and pleading, she kept her mother and father apart for a little while and felt in control. But he would always turn out the light. Peggy would turn it on and he would come back and turn it off — over and over again. *But* it kept her parents from fighting for a while. That was the whole point of the exercise.

In her therapy Peggy was asked what she had really wanted as a child. She said that she wanted her father to come in and hold her frightened, trembling little body, to calm her, to tell her he loved her and that it didn't matter that she had screamed. She wanted to know she was safe. She didn't want to be grown-up and deal with the fear.

So many Adult Child Mourners tell of their night terrors. They speak of the insecure yearning to feel safe. They recall the perplexities of simply not understanding what was happening. Somehow everything seemed worse in the darkness. In the light of day, even though situations rarely improved, it felt safer.

I, on the other hand, preferred the rich black velvet of night. It was easier to hide.

4

The Adult Child Syndrome

I teach a course called "The Adult Child Syndrome." One section is dedicated to the grieving process, dealing with the problems specified in the title of this book.

The Adult Child Syndrome refers to people who missed out on their childhood because they lived with severe dysfunction. The list is endless:

- Perfectionism
- Enforced religion
- Pathological gambling
- Mental illness
- Death of a sibling
- Long-term illness of a family member
- Emotional void
- Addictions
- Abuse

- Incest
- Imprisonment of a parent
- Death of parents
- Adoption
- Fostering
- Negativity

I'm sure you can add to it.

One group of participants in this course was willing to have the session recorded. I am grateful to them for this gracious gesture and their permission to include the transcript here.

The group was comprised of four men and eight women. The men ranged in age from 30 to 45: one businessman, one carpenter and two counselors. The women ranged in age from 22 to 50: one student, three businesswomen, two teachers and two counselors. To maintain their anonymity, all statements are simply identified by M=Male and F=Female and Y=Yvonne (me).

The subject of grieving created great fear and apprehension among some of the members. This excerpt from the workshop shares their statements, questions and concerns.

Yvonne: This situation of grieving a childhood that never was is difficult. Although it is heartbreaking and painful to grieve something that was, it's much more difficult to grieve something that wasn't, because you don't know what you've missed. It's a situation where you are trying to create something and you don't know what it is. A happy childhood? What is a happy childhood? What does that mean? Does that mean anything to anybody? Do you know what a happy childhood is?

Female: I thought I did.

Male: I did. It's free of problems. I transferred that over to today. When I don't have a problem, I'm happy. So when there wasn't any crisis in the house, that's when I was happy. Of course, that didn't happen too often.

Y: What I want to do is go through the grieving process with you and ask you some questions I learned from Elisabeth Kubler-Ross dealing with terminal illness. That's how I regard addictions, mental illness, whatever any of you dealt with, growing up.

Here is Dr. Kubler-Ross' list of the process of grieving:

1. Denial
2. Anger
3. Bargaining
4. Depression
5. Acceptance

What we need to start off with is to look at those areas and find out what they are. Then we can put them in the context of the Adult Child Syndrome.

Denial and isolation, or denial—what does that mean to you?

F: Of things the way they were.

Y: If you're thinking of grieving, what are you denying?

F: Denial of a loss.

Y: If you did react when something was going on in your family, what happened to you? If you showed emotion in your family, what happened to you?

F: You were told not to feel that way.

Y: Anything else? Was anybody punished for showing emotion?

F: Anger—sure. I was punished for saying no.

F: I was told that I didn't feel that way.

Y: Doesn't that happen in your adult life too?

F: Yeah. I find that I do that to other people.

F: If you're told that you don't feel that way, is it minimizing it?

Y: Absolutely. They're minimizing it and they're also protecting themselves. If you feel that way, they may have to deal with you.

It's *not nice!* That is another thing.

They have this wonderful thing, I don't know if they still do it in elementary schools—the magic circle. You've heard of that?

You have this magic circle. The children are given group rules. They are not allowed to interrupt each other. They can't talk about it outside the magic circle no matter what happens. The teacher will come up with an idea by saying, "We have a big box here today. What would you like to put in the box?"

A kid might say, "My brother. In pieces. Bit by bit."

Now a normal reaction from an adult to that child is what? "Don't say that about your brother. You don't mean that." However, that child might have been beaten up by his brother before he left home and that's exactly what he means. The teacher will not interrupt. He will just let him say it.

There's been a study done that showed when the magic circle is played, kids were able to concentrate better. They did their work. They felt more at peace because they "said it." I'm sure the child would be devastated if his brother was really in the box in pieces. That's not the point. The point was that he was given the freedom to express it in a controlled environment without someone saying, "That's not nice. You don't feel that way."

Now I pick up on that because I know that's why an awful lot of people don't deal with their adult child issues. Because it's not nice. It's not right. It's disloyal. It's this and it's that. Really we're talking about facts here. The fact is that that child is angry with his brother. He's only in first grade and he doesn't know how to verbalize it in any other way. But the rage is there. If we suppress that in children, they are going to grow up being adult children who don't know what to do with their feelings. It could be that this child comes from a background of a no-talk family: He's not allowed to "say it" anywhere. At least as a little child in the magic circle he can begin to identify what those feelings are.

Denial is a major protection. People can stay in it forever and still function. For example, the families of soldiers missing in action—they stay there. They don't believe their sons or daughters are dead out in Vietnam. They don't believe that. They don't see anything in the paper and there's no proof. So why should they? They function and they live their lives but they are in denial constantly. They'll tell you that.

M: What does that do to their immune system if there's this constant contradiction in a body?

Y: They get sick. People get sick. There's been a lot of study and research on the physical condition of the adult child. Most of them have a lot of lower back pain, intestinal problems, migraines, chest pain. There's a whole lot of it because you're repressing and you've got the strain, the stress and the tension. It's got to come out some way.

All of this is happening in this process, and the reason it's so incredibly complicated is that people don't know what they're grieving. If you've lost someone you love to death, you know what you're grieving. When I left my country, I knew what I was grieving. There were no two ways about it. My homesickness wasn't anything other than I wanted to be in England. That was it, in the early days.

When it's something that I don't know, when I feel this void, this nothingness here, but I don't know what it is, that makes it doubly difficult. Some smart person is going to say, "Well, what's the matter?"

"I don't know" I'm going to say.

"Well, look at yourself. You should feel fine." *Should?!*

I counseled a young woman just before I came here who is the youngest sister of a murder victim. And "everything's fine." I just looked at her. Everything is fine. I asked her, "Why do you think your mother asked you to come here?"

"I have no idea. No idea! But it's nice to meet you at last."

It's going to take us months because the pain of the reality is so terrible for this young woman that she is keeping herself here where it's safe. She is petrified to accept the death of her sister.

Denial isn't always negative. The reason we've made it to whatever stage we are, in this room, has been that we've learned to deal with these things. Our denial gave us the kind of protection we needed at that time because we weren't strong enough then to handle what we need to handle. I believed that even before I was in the program. I believe that the Higher Power really prepares us for things at any given time that we need to deal with. We don't have it until we're ready. That's why denial is valuable. Somewhere there's been a sudden death or a sudden situation, maybe a terminal illness was diagnosed, and this denial goes up. It's helpful at that time for people to feel numb. It's okay.

How long we stay in it and how it affects our lives, that's a whole different situation. That is something we need to look at. Whichever way you're looking at the situation of your childhood, you're all out of denial to a certain extent, or you wouldn't be here.

Anger. Anger is a very important emotion. When people get angry in recovery that's when I'm most comfortable, because I know they are not going to stay in denial and they're not going to go down without a fight.

If they don't deal with the anger, it becomes depression. That's what depression is—internalized emotions, especially love and anger. Those are the two emotions we don't know anything about as we're growing up. We don't know the difference between hurt, sensitivity, anger and rage.

I heard "no." I heard "don't trust." I heard "be careful who you reach out to," "don't let people touch you." We have a lot of negative messages around those two things.

"Don't wear your heart on your sleeve." Were you told that? "Nice girls don't get angry."

"The more you can drink or the more you can use your fist, that shows what a man you are." Men often deal with anger that way. So we have a whole lot of distorted memories and messages. You have a situation where two people are fighting and screaming and the kid asks, "Are you angry?"

They shout, *"No, I'm not angry!"*

Anyone with that loud voice usually scares the hell out of the children. Then they are beating up on each other and stay together and say they love each other. What kind of message does a child get?

It's not always loud stuff. It's not always physical abuse. It can be silence, not responding, just being nothing, not giving an opinion. There's all kinds of things.

F: Quite some time ago, it had to be at least 15 years ago, there was a psychologist on television. It really stuck in my mind what she said because it's exactly the way I grew up. She said parents can give children messages that are *positive-pos-*

itive. Like everything is wonderful. Or they can give them negative stuff all of the time. She said the worst kind of message is a positive with a negative because it is so confusing. That's what I always got: "You're smart but you're sloppy."

Y: "You're smart, but you're not trying."

F: I never got just one thing. Never.

Y: Here's an example of pull-push control. I have a young woman I'm working with now who is in a severely dysfunctional family, very positive-positive. The parents are willing to send her to school, to do everything, as long as she goes to the school they want her to go to. As long as she achieves the goals that they want her to. That's not unconditional love. That's something we don't know. We don't know unconditional love. We don't know total acceptance. We need to learn total acceptance of yourself to yourself because you're always going to live with you.

F: I'm confused now because when I was little, I was either happy or sad. When I went out, I was happy. When I was in, I was sad. I was only sad because my mother and father were sad. If they had had a fight and I would go to them, they would always be nice to me. They would always hug me and tell me they were sorry that I was sad. I think what I got out of it was that nothing can be fixed. Maybe that's why I never, ever told them my problems because I knew that they couldn't fix their own. They were loving and giving people, but there was no way they could fix themselves. So that's why I end up thinking that I don't know what I am doing.

Y: Negativity is contagious. Even though they tell you how much they love you, if you're surrounded by that atmosphere, it's going to go right into your pores. When you get well, you are going to revolt against that.

M: You just reminded me of something. I don't tell people my problems. I think I learned that from my parents. I never went to my father or mother and said, "I have a problem. Will you help me?"

Y: What's sad about it?

M: Because we thought that they couldn't help us?

F: How could they help us when they couldn't help themselves?

Y: There's a lack of trust.

F: I knew they were trying hard, but that wasn't denial of love for me. I don't know what was the matter. I just know that they weren't happy and I wasn't happy because they weren't happy.

Y: As a little girl you would want to fix that.

F: I think I was unhappy right up until my father died. Then I never had to fix it anymore.

M: Plus the fact when we are small, we think it's our fault.

F: You know, I just can't really think . . .

Y: You're thinking as a woman now, as an adult. Get your head into a little girl who's looking at two big people in her life who are very, very sad. What's the little girl feeling? What does she see?

F: I wish that I could help her.

Y: What did you do to try and help her? It's really important. What did you do to try and help her?

F: I was trying to explain to the one what the other one meant.

Y: You still didn't get happy, did you? It didn't matter what this lovely little girl did, who cared so much about these two big people.

F: They told me they were sorry, though. They were sorry I had to be exposed to it.

Y: Why were they sad?

F: Because they just didn't get along at all.

Y: They didn't have what it took to get away from one another.

F: They couldn't get away. I remember that it was years later when I was older and we talked about it, my mother said, "I had no place to go and no money to go there."

I remember saying, "Why didn't you just get a divorce? After all, mothers are supposed to know what to do."

She said, "Where would you go? Where would you go with two kids and no money and no job?"

Y: I used to pray every night that my parents would get a divorce.

F: I used to pray that they wouldn't. I used to say, "Oh God, don't ever let them die or anything because they had us."

I'm remembering something that I haven't thought about in years. My mother used to say that she prided herself in knowing her children's faults. I suppose she was very happy. That's all we heard . . . our faults. Nothing else.

Y: Did you marry somebody like that?

F: Yes.

Y: So did I. I never knew what was wrong. Isn't that amazing? I just remembered that. It's painful stuff, isn't it?

It's the negativity. We don't realize how incredibly contagious it is and we get mates who are the same as our parents.

Y: So what do we do? We think, "It must be me. It's got to be me. It can't be him or her."

M: What you are saying just triggered something in my own head. One incident I can focus on very, very clearly as if it just happened yesterday. My father came home and he was drunk. My parents then had a tremendous argument. I remember my father chasing me upstairs because I wanted to stay with them. He chased me up to the bed and I can still see him standing there. He was going to hit me and he never, ever hit me before. He didn't hit me. He went out of the room. I felt then that he should hit me and get it over with rather than to go through the same thing over and over, again and again. Because I knew next week it was going to be the same thing. Next Sunday we're going to go through the same thing.

Y: You had the Sunday syndrome in your house?

M: Yes. Sunday.

Y: Sunday syndrome. Did he have a migraine headache?

M: No . . . I'm not sure. He would just come in and go to bed. From Monday to Friday he never drank. Saturday he would drink a little. On Sunday he would get up very early and go to service, come home, say, "Hello. Hello. Bye, bye." and then go to the pub. We wouldn't see him until around 1:00. He would come in and be very sloppily drunk.

Part of this I am aware of. That's why I have a problem with certain foods. It's an addiction. The whole business of trying to mediate what they were doing. Trying to solve that. Trying to resolve, negotiate that.

Y: How many of you tried to keep the peace between your parents?

F: I still do with my children.

Y: This one, the bargaining, what do you think that is? We just talked about it, briefly.

F: "If I can just get them to be quiet and listen to one another, it's going to be okay."

Y: The bargaining can also be part of the denial. It throws up these levels of protection that we have so we don't have to look at the problem. We'll say, "It wasn't that bad! Come on. It's not so bad."

F: It *was* that bad and I have to recognize how bad it was, so I don't have to think about it anymore. I can let it go.

M: I think it's interesting that a lot of times in the same family, like my sister is five years older than me, and she said it wasn't that bad. I hear that a lot in programs and around different places.

Y: The fact is that siblings in the same family will have different perceptions entirely. In Robert Ackerman's book, *Same House, Different Homes*, he looks at the brothers and sisters who look at the situation differently, from people saying, "They are falling down drunk," to, "He drinks?" It's that extreme.

F: That's the way it was in my family. When I talk to my brother and sister about problems, they both remember a very happy childhood. I said, "Don't you remember all the yelling?" And they don't.

So then I start thinking that maybe it wasn't that bad. Maybe I was just overly sensitive. I can't make all that up. I still go back into minimizing it for myself and denying it.

Y: You take that into your adult life today. How much credibility do you give other people for telling you what you think, who you are, what you feel, that you are wrong, that you are right, that you're good, that you're bad, that you're angry, that you're not. How much credibility can you give people?

F: If they give me negative, I think "Exactly, that's it." If they give me positive, I think they don't see me or that's not right.

Y: That's the imposter syndrome that we live with. But that whole aspect of saying, "I have to say to you . . ." Next time someone says that, accuses you of something, stop and think. Are they right or are they wrong? Sometimes they are and sometimes they're not. The adult child is going to swallow the whole thing and say they are right.

F: It happened on Friday when somebody accused me of doing stuff, I stopped and thought about it.

I was able to deal with it at the time, but all weekend I kept thinking. "Oh, I'm horrible. I'm not good." It was real painful.

Y: There is a very simple way of dealing with that. As I told you, we are going to go right to recovery, right from the start. What do you do when people criticize you? Just agree with them. It knocks them right on their ass!

"You're a very angry woman!" "Right!" Do you keep responding to people who do that to you? You are telling them that they are right but, "I'm not going to defend myself to you."

You don't have to. We spend 75 percent of our life defending things we don't have to defend. It is exhausting. I mean, we get tired. Adult children get tired. We suffer from fatigue because we do all this dancing and prancing around. It takes time. I taught my children this: There is no need to be defensive. Instead of defending, we simply agree.

For example, "You know, you're really an angry bitch." "Well, I try."

What are they going to do? There is nothing they can do.

Years ago when I first started in my recovery, to be honest I would have to attack. I don't have to do that anymore, I just state how I feel, very calmly, with my voice no different than it is now.

F: Even stating how you feel in many situations and relationships is going to cause problems in areas you're not going to be able to deal with.

F: You've got to be able to face it. To be honest about your feelings.

Y: **Depression.** There is so much confusion with this word. Any high school student taking a "potpourri of problems" course will want to check into a hospital when this disorder is discussed. However, in grieving the word is *sadness.* What are your feelings regarding that word?

M: I didn't know what it was until I was an adult. I used to throw up a lot and have tight feelings in my stomach when I

was blamed for everything that happened in the family. It
didn't matter whether I was there or not!

F: It was a sinking feeling in my stomach. I know now it
was the utter helplessness—being the total victim. At that time
it was numbness.

M: I don't like the word even today, in recovery. It says, "I
should pull myself together. What do I have to be sad for? I've
got my act in order!"

Y: You are speaking as an adult. The child is still sad.

F: I suppose I first felt sad when I went to my best friend's
house. Her family was so warm and welcoming I wanted
them to adopt me. They didn't, and I thought that was because
I wasn't good enough.

Y: How did you accept that you were?

F: It's still going on—this acceptance thing.

M: Acceptance means giving in and I can't. I want my childhood even though logically I can't have it. I want to be nur-
tured and cared for, to be accepted absolutely.

(At this point, this man cried bitterly, mourning the loss of
he knew not what. The words were there—the full impact was
apparent. He was on the journey.)

F: This is too painful for me—I'm leaving.

Y: Like always. Fight or flight. Just come and sit with me, and
hold your child closely. You are an adult and your child is
scared—afraid of people's emotions. Tell her she won't be hurt
and that one day soon, she will be able to do what he is doing.

F: Thank you. (She began to rock and croon softly.)
Ten-minute break for hugging.

Y: When we talk about grief as a child and now as an adult
child, what were you or are you grieving?

F: Happy family.

M: Being loved unconditionally.

F: I didn't know what I was grieving until someone else just
said it.

Y: What you're grieving really is no memories.

F: I think I spent my life trying to create a family because
I probably didn't have one, and we still can't do it.

Y: So it's fantasy really, isn't it?

F: I'm still grieving grandparents and people. One of the things I did wrong on my time line. My grandmother's death is still a very big issue.

Y: Is it possible that that's where you got your unconditional love?

M: I just started grieving that. She was the only one I really cared about in the family.

F: I was the perfect child.

M: Memories—when you mentioned about the grandparents—this one man in my life, my grandfather, was incredibly effective. His death just threw me into absolute confusion. I didn't know how to behave. And it's all coming back, trying to write all this stuff down.

F: I didn't have grandparents. They were all dead. My parents died and part of me is grieving. It's a part that's not there that other people have.

Y: Have you no history? I feel like that, being an only child and living in another country. When I went back to England with my brother-in-law and sister-in-law, it suddenly went "click." I didn't realize how many people loved me. I love people in this country but they cannot share my history. That's a big thing with you. You don't have parents and you grieve the history.

F: I can grieve and I'm still grieving the fact that I never had any brothers and sisters. I remember as a child wanting nothing more than another human being around besides me, just to take the burden off my shoulders. I can remember feeling this as a little girl.

Y: A lot of children really respond to those commercials where a child is sick and both parents are there taking care of them. The school nurses' offices are jammed. Kids see that's the way to get attention. They watch television, see the commercials and they get sick. Children make themselves sick to try and create that. Even though it doesn't happen.

M: When I went into treatment for cocaine, I realized that wasn't the real problem. My addiction was getting headaches so I could take pills where I could get attention.

Y: If we can't get positive, then we get negative, as long as we get attention. It doesn't matter what kind it is as long as we get it.

F: You know the song "Memories" from *Cats?* Every time I hear that it strikes such a chord. I cry. It's spontaneous. There's a part there that says, "Touch me. It's so easy to leave me, all alone with my memories." I never really understood that, but I just feel so alone. I guess I'm grieving, I don't know what. It's something. I don't know whether it's acceptance or love. I really feel alone and that I'm grieving. I don't know what it is.

Y: Grieving could be that possibility of just not having anyone you really feel understood by. Of not being able to share what's really deep inside of you because maybe they just wouldn't understand, and so you keep yourself just caught up in that by not risking it.

I think there's a connection in being held and accepted unconditionally. I think a lot of adult children feel it. I know I certainly did. Of course, I wasn't okay. I was in a ruined state and I was not wanted at all.

The difficult thing about this is to honestly look at where you feel the dysfunction was. I can see it happening right now with you.

"I'm not touching on it now."

"I haven't hit it yet."

That's the feeling. The fact that I haven't hit on it yet is the feeling. Because nobody understood and nobody can get exactly what you are trying to say.

I have one patient who constantly says to me, "Yvonne, you don't understand. You don't understand."

A lot of that is her resistance and her defense. If I understood, what else would she have? She would have to share that real mystique about her if I understood.

F: I have a very dear friend whom I feel does understand me totally.

Y: Just think about this—because a lot of adult children feel different, we want to be special. Sometimes if people understand that we are special, we lose the mystique. Just think about it. Let it sit there for a while.

What have we got to complain about? What defense mechanism?

I had a grieving situation about four weeks ago. I had one of those days where nothing was right. I went to a restaurant and they didn't know how to run the restaurant. I went to a meeting and the speaker didn't know what the hell he was talking about. Sitting in that meeting I suddenly realized that I was grieving over having nothing left to grieve. I had nothing to blame anymore. Anything that happens to me is my responsibility now. That's one hell of a burden. I gave up the grief. I've been grieving most of my life for these things, and now I have to grieve that I don't have that anymore.

A lot of the times we keep ourselves caught in the pain, the dysfunction, whatever. Because that's how we used to deal with it. What you are looking at is change. That is very frightening to all of us.

F: How about grieving for normalcy? I'd love to be normal—if I knew what it was. All I know is what I think it is: to be loved, listened to, touched, worried over, concerned for, missed, stroked, encouraged, applauded, guided, directed, given some stability and purpose. Can we get it, Yvonne?

Y: You betcha! Keep on believing!

5

Role Models: From Television To Reality

We speak frequently of having no healthy role models when we were children. Certainly what and who we considered "normal," in retrospect, were usually people close to us who were trying to survive their own lifestyle problems.

I began to realize that I was different, when I felt that the *Addams Family* and the *Munsters* were normal. On viewing *The Brady Bunch* and, in recent years, *The Cosby Show,* I experienced discomfort and anger. Looking into these feelings, I discovered that the Bradies and Cosby showed supposedly "normal" families working *all* problems to a satisfactory resolution. Somehow, I never felt it to be real—it was all too pat. The only show I watch now that approaches normal is *Roseanne,* and even that is a little too slick in response. The beauty of "Roseanne" is that so many of us would have put up with the sarcasm and the facetiousness if it had been done with the warmth, love and affection shown on the little screen.

Maybe I don't think the *Addams Family* and the *Munsters*
are exactly normal today, but I still believe these programs
were the first to show unconditional family love. These two
families accepted each member without question. The love,
anger and disappointment were all expressed. They certainly
knew all about forgiveness. Today I watch these programs
with warm delight. I have learned and tried to teach that role
models do not have to look or behave in any special way
other than nonjudgmentally. In these shows none of the
members of the family accepted unacceptable behavior, but
none of the children were loved simply because they had a
good report card. They were loved—period. If there were
problems, the love wasn't affected.

I'm sure that loving these two families makes me "different,"
yet when I think of them as role models, there is a sweet
nostalgia that causes me to smile. No, I don't float around in
gauze and have long black hair. My significant other doesn't
swoon with ecstacy when I use French words. Yet I feel the
security of those families, and if that's what a role model is
supposed to be, I'm an Addams Munster.

Other television models aren't so happy. Commercials can
create an ideal family situation that is unreal to Adult Child
Mourners. Behaviors like those of children in these ads were
not tolerated in their families of origin, nor would they be in
most normal families today. Commercials showing children
deliberately dropping food on the floor or pulling cloths from
tables laden with food and looking gleeful just don't register.
Sometimes a cough or a sneeze would have brought a blow
to the head in their families. Compare that to the commercial
where the child has a fever and both parents rush to the
bedside to offer comfort. Most Adult Child Mourners will
share that they dared not be sick. Some were punished for it.
I know I used it for attention, even though it was negative.
School nurses will attest to the fact that their rooms are
jammed on Monday mornings with children wanting attention
from someone who will treat them kindly.

Many Adult Child Mourners have serious physical problems
brought on by the need for attention. Some of them were
never touched as children except through violence, so the

pattern of behavior to attract negativity sets in at a very young age. Sadly, adults don't realize that these survival skills no longer work and only grief and pain ensue if they continue to attract negativity. These people frequently end up lonely and neglected because the pattern is so ingrained. They are hypochondriacal and miserable. No one wants to be around them. They seem unable to summon the strength to change the attitudes that brought them to this despairing plight. They cannot conceive that they created it. Trying to exist without someone to blame is impossible for such people. They are pitiful, pathetic and hopeless. Some, however, have learned that it is never too late to change. With extreme courage, they have entered recovery and renewed their lives to become happy, productive people.

What any Adult Child Mourner has to do is dispel the myths of childhood. Their sick parents lied to them about feelings and emotions; lied to them about their basic human rights; lied to them about relationships.

What were your role models? They were not always people—they were often unspoken messages created by observing the behavior between the Big People in the family. Did you believe that love had to hurt? Did you believe that if you were angry with someone, you didn't love them and vice versa? Did you believe that you had to please everybody in order to be happy and live a good life? Did you believe that you had to like everybody? Were you taught that you had to be all things to your man? Were you taught that you had to earn more money than your woman? Make your own list and check with your first chart.

When the Adult Child Mourner begins to exit slowly from that inner fortress, the memories of the old role models begin to emerge. These models, together with the self-inflicted sabotage, the back and forth, the push me/pull me patterns, create havoc. Know now that this is the beginning of the Adult Child Mourner creating his or her own role models and normality.

Each time the adult ventures forth, an old message pops up and the child retreats. As treatment becomes a reality, the retreats become shorter and the realization of the reactions come more quickly. At times the retreat is caught en route. A recognition of people, places and things is born. The recovering adult child develops a conscious knowledge that for example, "when I'm here with her at this restaurant talking about the past, I slip right back into that passive/aggressive behavior. When that happens, I pick up a drink or food to 'fix' my feelings of despair."

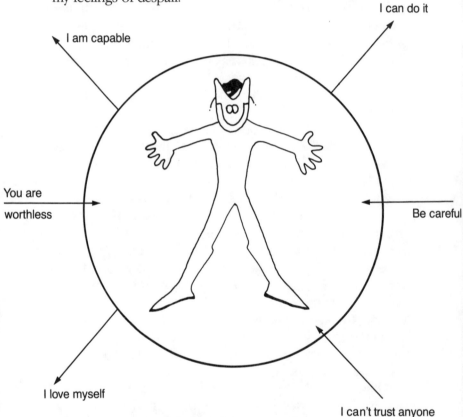

Figure 5.1. Mixed Messages

In addition to having negative role models, children who had no childhood learn to take responsibility for the failure. "It was my fault" or "I deserved it" are comments frequently heard when Adult Child Mourners are attempting to defend their non-childhood. They minimize, insisting, "It wasn't *that*

bad!" Each time they do that, they push another layer of
denial and guilt further into their mind.

At this point the Adult Child Mourner has to make a definite move. Examining the past has been an important part
of the preparation for recovery. Dwelling on it, however,
stifles the necessary growth process. Moving beyond it is a
difficult transition. It is hard for people who had a normal
childhood to move from one developmental stage to another.
For a person who had no healthy frame of reference, it
seems almost impossible.

For years Piet tried to make some kind of sense of the
family in which she grew up. She is a writer who created page
after page of feelings, questions and disgust at trying so hard.
It never occurred to her until recently that possibly her parents
didn't want to have children—for the right reasons. She expressed her new and painful awareness thus . . .

I woke up in the middle of the night feeling the pain that
my brother must have gone through, getting beaten with a
belt. How he must have started to hate himself because he
was powerless to stop the beatings. So you hate yourself and
it still doesn't stop and you wish you were dead all the time.
You just want to die to stop the misery. *Why, why, why, why,
why* would any parent want to do that to his child? Even if
you don't like the kid, the kid never did anything to you.
Why would you want the kid to suffer when you've got to
know somewhere, sometime, the world is going to find out
about how you treated your kid and you will be held accountable for your actions? Someday you are going to suffer
as you have caused that child to suffer.

I remember one terrible time when we were all playing
or just hanging around in the kitchen and being noisy.
Ethan was standing on a kitchen chair. Dad was trying to
take a nap and he couldn't sleep. We were making too
much noise, I suppose. He came into the kitchen like a
lightning bolt and grabbed Ethan by the leg. He dragged
Ethan off the chair and through the dining room, with his
head banging on the floor the whole way, and then up the

stairs to his room, with his head banging on each step, until he threw him into bed. I ran after him because I couldn't believe my eyes. I had to make sure it really happened. There was Mom, lying on the couch with her head buried in the pillow, crying but not lifting a finger to help her son who was being tortured and possibly brain damaged for life. (To this day I wonder how it is that he didn't suffer any brain damage.) I still remember the sound of his head on the stairs, *thud, thud, thud.* I wasn't even scared to run after Dad and look, which was unusual for me. I was in a state of shock. I couldn't believe any human would do that to another, let alone my own father—that is hardly the word to describe him. This is tremendously upsetting to write about and remember. The tears are flowing. I realize how much I hate my mom. I look at her and think, "There's a worthless human being," and since I resemble Mom in some ways, I think I'm worthless, too.

Yvonne would say, "You're angrier at your mother than your father." I couldn't quite agree before, but now I know. I hate my father more, but I'm angrier at Mom. Because I feel nothing good for my father, but I still feel something for my mom. I expected her to do something for me, to help me. Of course she didn't. So hence all the anger.

I was crying, feeling the pain of realizing that my mother doesn't love me and never will. Not the way a mother should love her child, especially a gifted, sensitive child like myself. She is the person that I love most in the world and she will never love me. I'm realizing that she's not a beauteous bundle of love but a damaged person who doesn't even appreciate her own good points.

With all the beatings, I knew that Dad would kill us if he had the chance. How's that for a feeling of total insecurity?

Emotions in turmoil, that was my life. I had to learn self-love, self-acceptance, self-forgiveness. I am learning these and there's less turmoil in my life now.

All my life I've been tearing my hair out wondering, "How can Mom not care? How can she not be more interested in what's happening to her children—in the safety of her kids?" Every other mother I knew tried to do right by her children and wasn't afraid to be obvious about it. But not Mom. La-la-land all the way.

How can she love us and not care? She was always telling

us how much she cared. Her idea of caring was being strict
and punishing us (or making sure Dad punished us) or
berating me for every little thing.

So I realized that she doesn't love us at all. I don't think
I take this personally anymore at this point because she
doesn't love herself. Nobody loves her, and she doesn't
know what love is.

I woke up this morning feeling my usual anger and
hurt because my mother doesn't love me, and then it hit
me. I don't even like her. Come to think of it, she has very
few redeeming qualities that I can think of, outside of
giving birth to me. And she's probably a person that I
would not want to know or have much contact with. Is
this a minor miracle or what? I seem to have less of a
burden to carry around.

Piet is in therapy for her self-esteem. She attends workshops
and reads relevant material constantly. She is thirsty for ways
to discover her own *normal.* By recognizing the reality of her
parent's inadequacies, she is in the process of forgiveness.

To undo such destructive reactive behavior takes time. As is
said in some support meetings, put one foot in front of the
other. So it is with reconstructive education. It is a slow process. The problem of family loyalty always arises at this time.
This is when it is essential to eliminate the personalities involved and focus on the consistent learned behavior. This is
when "acting as if" is critical. This is when we say no to the
voices that remind us that we are no good, useless nuisances.
This is when we say to our destructive reminders, "Be quiet,
I'm getting better!"

Positive Influences List

When doing some work in a prison system, I asked the
prisoners to think of four people who had positively influenced their lives. I wanted an immediate reaction — the first
four, without thought or analysis. In the majority of cases, a
schoolteacher (usually kindergarten) appeared on that list.

Sometimes a kindly elderly person or a minister would show up. A minority included a parent or older sibling.

Please make such a list now for yourself and then continue to read.

This is an important exercise, as the Adult Child Mourner has no or very little memory on a conscious level of any people who were a positive influence. They remember only the pain and grief of those they relied on to be positive, who betrayed that faith—their parents the Big People.

When the list is complete, write as much as you can regarding the feelings you have about these people. It's good to do this with someone else, if possible, so all you have to do is talk and let the other person write what they hear you say. It is fascinating to discover that there were good role models in your life, the memory of whom was buried with the pain.

One of our greatest fears is that we will turn out like those who raised us, so we tend to overlook the people who helped us to survive. Take a look at the description you have of these treasured memories and see how many of their characteristics you have today.

Here is my own chart from 1968—the first I ever did.

Dr. Alex, Minister. He came into my life when I was 15. Quiet. Scholarly. Intelligent. Kind. Was not influenced by the demands of others. Could make choices. Had strong belief systems. Believed in me. Saw something in me I didn't see for another 30 years. Was totally accepting of me. Encouraged me to follow my philosophies.

Mrs. Harrison. She was an old Irish lady who lived in the flat beneath us. I wouldn't eat eggs for anyone but Mrs. Harrison. She was quiet and loving, very patient, and a port in the storm for me. I was three years old. She would listen and clap when I would sing and dance. Her son George and daughter Kathleen were also warm and loving to me, a frightened little girl. She would croon to me and rock me on her knee. I loved her without question.

Grandfather. Funny. Rough talking. His children were scared of him. I wasn't. He was a tailor. Would dress me in stiff petticoats and I would sit for hours on the front step with the greyhound dog and a small tin can. Each customer would drop pennies in my can. He would say, "She earns more money than me, this Shirley Temple." I felt so safe with him. He wouldn't allow anyone to criticize me. I was his Princess. I could do no wrong. (When he died, I was dethroned.)

Miss Alexander, French teacher. Taught me to dig into the depths. Was difficult. Irrational. Quite crazy. Taught me that I could do anything I chose to do, be anyone I wanted to be and have fun doing it. She taught with a flair. She was colorful, funny, a free spirit.

Look at all four examples and pick out the similarities in mine. They are so obvious. In another chapter I'll repeat this, with an up-to-date influence chart. You can do these as often as you like.

When I wrote this last time about my grandfather, I cried, and that's okay, too, even though it happened over 50 years ago. Delayed grief is something from which most of us suffer.

Do your chart now. Discuss it with someone you trust to help recognize the positives in your role models.

When you have completed this task, read on. I have expanded my descriptions of my four key people and the exercise has brought warmth, joy and fond memories. For a long time I didn't know I had any.

When engrossed in the pain of grieving the childhood that never was, Adult Child Mourners tend to overlook the rare positives. To recognize them in recovery is important, as it helps us accept beautiful friendships and love relationships to which we have a right. When I think of these four people I cry, I laugh, my heart lightens. I know that my God did then what It does now — put people in my life to guide me and help me grow.

Dr. Alex was a bachelor. In the Jewish community, unmarried rabbis were frowned upon. I don't know if that is still the case because I no longer follow any organized religion. Dr. Alex was a scholar, a private man with a passion for literature and religion. He was no social butterfly. The ladies of the Guild did all they could to matchmake, but he wanted nothing to do with it. He was a kind and gentle man, probably the most open-minded man of the cloth I had ever encountered. He communicated well with young people, especially those of us who were shy and insecure. At the age of 15 I was covered with acne. My nose used to turn red at the very thought of cold weather. I saw myself as tall for my age, skinny and unattractive. People would say, "She's a very nice girl once you get to know her."

I was fairly popular "once you got to know me" because I would do anything to please. Dr. Alex knew that beneath the fixed, "What can I do for you?" smile lay much pain and confusion. He knew what was going on at home, though I could never make out just how he knew. He introduced me to the study of comparative religion and was a major part of my classical education. (Whenever I answer well, watching *Jeopardy!* I thank him!) Dr. Alex helped me to recognize a faint glimmer of my own intelligence—very faint, but there. He also saw in me something that took another 25 years for me to see. He saw leadership and compassion. I had no idea what he meant, but he helped give me a fundamental belief in a Power greater than myself.

Mrs. Harrison. Everybody should have a Mrs. Harrison, a typical Irish mother. How I loved her. When I hear all the hatred today, I often wonder what she would have thought. Mrs. Harrison lived in the flat below us when I was small. She had two grown children. Kathleen lived with her and George came home from time to time when he was on leave. Oh, he was so handsome in his Army uniform. When he would carry me on his shoulder, I felt like a goddess. Mrs. Harrison was the person who taught me to cuddle. I didn't like to eat eggs, but as this was a prewar period, we could buy eggs cheaply. My mother would send me downstairs with two eggs (they had to be brown) and Mrs. Harrison and I would consume them with Hovis brown bread and marmalade. (My mouth waters at the memory.) I would dress up and sing for her. What fun we had! But the best, the very best, was the cuddling, the rocking, the crooning when I wouldn't sleep.

After the war I traced her to Streatham in South London, where she had moved after being bombed out. I used to go visit her, dragging a suitcase full of clothes on the bus so I could dress up to give her a concert. One day I went with my friend Jill. There was no answer, and I never saw her again. Because of all the joy and the love she gave me, I never thought she had left. As my colleague Thom Murgitroyde puts it so well: "Real love requires no effort."

Mrs. Harrison lived in my heart, even when there was no reply. She is alive and well now, especially when I feel joy. She'll never leave or die.

Grandfather. How does a child describe God? That's what he was to me. He was funny, outrageous, controlling, a child. My grandmother was beautiful but a demanding martinet in her own right. He would "yes, dear" her and do what he wanted. As an immigrant, his knowledge of the English language was sparse at first. Then he discovered certain words.

In England the word "sod" is unacceptable. Back in the '30s it was unheard of to use such profanity. It is a shortened form of "sodomy." So if it were used as a descriptive adjective or a statement, it was absolutely not "nice." My grandfather used to dictate letters to my Uncle Joe if any organization or merchant had incurred his displeasure. He would state the company name and, "Dear Sir, Sod you." I can recall people howling with laughter when my grandfather would respond to "Where is your wife?" by stating, "The old cow is in the kitchen," thinking it was a term of endearment.

He loved me without question. He was tough to his children, but with me he was totally, unconditionally loving. I was five when he died. I've promised myself that one day I'll write a book about my family, Grandpa in particular.

Miss Alexander was the first eccentric I ever knew. The woman loved France and the French language with a passion. She told us from the start that it would be a miracle if anyone got any grade higher than a *C* in her class, and this was the year that we had to take a national examination which would have an impact on our future. She was impossible. We never knew what to expect. She dressed in her own inimitable fashion, which in our knowledgeable 16-year-old minds were peculiar at best. She wore the brightest multicolored shoes. When she entered the classroom, everyone would surreptitiously strain to see what she had on her feet, at which point she would leap onto the top of her desk and pirouette with her feet high in the air.

"And now," she would announce, "we can get on with the impossible task of teaching you French."

Forget telling her you hadn't done your homework. A firing squad would have been easier. Because of her demanding instruction, I gained a distinction in French in the national examination. Miss Alexander taught me the reality of life, that I could learn if I chose to. Yes, she was difficult, but she never singled anyone out, never name-called, never derided except all of us together. Her attitude, bizarre as it was, was fun—and I learned it was up to me.

These four people taught me a lot that I didn't fully utilize until years later. All of them were positive forces for me over 40 years ago.

The object of this exercise is that the assets you have listed are those to which you react positively today. If you do not recognize them within yourself, with treatment, it is merely a matter of time. They are there. They are the tools which will provide for you — life after survival. They are the "where-to-from-here" methods of joy, potential and permanent emotional wellness. Enjoy them.

6

What Is Normal Grieving?

This question frequently pops up when the discussion centers around the word *normal*. What is normal grieving? It is multifaceted and all moves toward healing and recovery.

Normal grieving, as opposed to the grief over a dysfunctional family, is due to something known and something lost. What do normal people grieve? Everything that causes a major change, usually against the wishes of the person concerned. People grieve the following:

- Death
- Divorce
- Separation
- Leaving home
- Moving
- Leaving friends
- Losing a game
- Illness
- Losing hair

Make your own list.

Normal is to go through the stages of grief until it becomes healing. Normal people do not question or suppress their pain and anguish at the loss, whatever it is. They process it in some or all of the following ways:

- They will seek help by talking with a trusted friend, a minister or a professional therapist.
- They might join a therapy group or go to a support group.
- They will not be afraid to cry and talk about the loss.
- They will *want* to heal themselves.
- They will not want to stay in their misery.
- They understand that the pain will stay for a while because they loved whoever or whatever they lost and that loss hurts.
- They do not go on long-term medication.
- They feel their pain and know it to be normal.
- They give themselves a period of time and then return to work.
- They acknowledge their grief.
- They know whom they can trust.
- They know they are powerless.
- They get well in their own time.
- They are very honest in their feelings.
- They know it takes time to recover.
- They know it wasn't their fault; or if a part was their fault, they own it.
- They do not beat themselves up.
- They do not endlessly grieve what was.
- They acknowledge that grief is a part of living and that death is a part of the life cycle.

The levels of grieving as composed by Elisabeth Kubler-Ross in her classic work *On Death And Dying* are as follows:

1. Denial and isolation
2. Anger
3. Bargaining
4. Depression
5. Acceptance

Dr. Kubler-Ross came to create these components in her work with terminally ill patients. She saw that there were levels of grieving experienced both by the patients and their loved ones. This is a normal process. The only word I challenge in her list is *depression*. I prefer *sadness* because that is a normal feeling when someone we love is lost to death or is dying. The fact that our culture doesn't like sadness and constantly tries to cheer people up is the kind of denial to which we have referred earlier in this book.

In normal grieving there is very little guilt. The "if onlys" do not have a long life span when confronted with normality. They shrivel up quickly because they are of no value to recovery. Normal people understand that grieving is a process — a process of recovery that works in conjunction with the willingness of the mourner. See how this attitude varies from that of the Adult Child Mourner. There is little blame or shame, guilt or reproach among healthy grieving people. Their happy, stable childhood prepared them for death and loss. These are the people who are taught a healthy respect for articles, for books, for other people's belongings. They learned that all people were different in some way and that was perfectly acceptable. They lived with people who allowed and encouraged the precious gift of childhood.

What Is A Happy Childhood?

What then is a happy childhood? It's taken me over 50 years to discover it, and I am all the list I'll give you. It is my honest desire to help you recover a lot more quickly than I did. Remember, throughout all of this reading, recovery is possible and permanent. It's up to you whether you want it!

What Are The Components?

Primarily, a child has to feel safe, fed, clothed and sheltered. There has to be responsible communication. The child needs to be touched, kissed, stroked and told, "You are a miracle."

There has to be laughter. Direction. Teaching what's right and what is wrong. Problems must be explained. There should be an understanding that because life is somewhat difficult, there are alternatives, options and choices. Happy children know there is a Big Person who will help out. To protect is not the answer. To teach a child how to interact at all levels is essential. Happy children are well mannered. They care about others but know their boundaries. How are they taught those?

It is a common mistake to believe that children can be taught boundaries by anything other than example. Remember that Adult Child Mourners have extremely difficult role models whose examples were disastrous. As a result, Mourners are afraid of the way they raise their own children. Normal children recognize boundaries by being treated with kindness, firmness and respect.

Although it is a great temptation to launch into "the raising of children," it is inappropriate at this stage as the important focus is on the reader of this book.

An English author, Charles Kingsley, wrote in his book *The Water Babies* of a lady whose name was "Mrs. Do-as-you-would-be-done-by." He said, "Mutual respect is the keynote of any responsible relationship." For example: "Do you know where your children are?" is as important as "Do your children know where you are?" It is important not to demand from them what you are not willing to do or give. It is so simple to leave a note telling them where you can be reached if necessary.

"I never knew where my parents were after I was about four years old," says Manny, the oldest of seven children. "All I knew was that they seemed to be around for a while, then a new baby would appear and off they'd go again. Grief? Sure, I know grief — being the 'man of the house' from four years of age, whenever they both took off. Was it any wonder that I never knew how to be a kid? Fun — what's that? When I read about people having a wonderful childhood with their large family, I want to punch walls. I was changing diapers when I was four years old. My kids are all addicted because I didn't let them do anything — no housework, no work. I gave them generous allowances, bought their cars. I tried so hard to have them enjoy a happy childhood that I completely forgot to be human. I worked to provide them with the things I never had. I *was not* going to be like my parents. In one way I was just like them. By working so hard to get these things, I stole time from my kids' growing years. We were all robbed of our childhood." Manny and his family have since entered treatment. They are in the process of recovery, finding that *normal* isn't that far away. They are learning about loving oneself so others can be loved and accepted. It isn't easy, but it is simple.

The Importance Of Pets

Children learn a great deal, having pets. It's sad when parents don't permit them. "I can remember my dad, in one of his irrational rages, throwing a puppy across the room," recalls Alison. "My father was insanely jealous of anything or anyone who received attention, especially from me or my mother. He would go quite mad for days. I learned that it wasn't safe to have pets because they might get hurt. If any of them died, they were wrapped up and put in the garbage." Alison continues, "I thought that Big People were supposed to comfort and make everything all right. When my cat died and I cried, my father went beserk. I didn't know what to do, so I just went to my room and cried, cried and cried."

Bill told me that as a child he was incredibly lonely. His siblings had nothing to do with him, treating him as the male version of Cinderella. They lived on a tiny farm with a cow, a pig, a couple of goats and a few chickens for eggs. When he was about 10, Bill took two of the newly-hatched chicks and raised them as pets. They were the only source of love he had. They would come to him when he called their names. They were very important living things in his life. When he came home from school, he would always call them and then do his mountain of chores. He came home late one day, called his pets and they didn't come. He ran everywhere looking, calling — nothing! He went into the kitchen to ask his mother if she had seen the chickens. As usual, she ignored him. Bill was frantic. Finally he set about doing his chores before being called in to dinner.

"Yvonne, you have no idea of the horror I felt seeing two roasted chickens come out of the oven — I just knew. I know as a 44-year-old man that people would laugh, but my throat still contracts when I think of that episode. When I screamed at my parents, knowing those chickens were my pets, do you know what they did? They laughed. My brothers and sisters (knowing what was good for them) laughed, too. I have never felt so alone and devastated since that time, even though I have endured terrible situations — I still don't eat chicken."

So what is normal grieving and where does it fit in with a happy childhood? First and foremost, normal families recognize children's sensitivities. Children learn to accept that death is a normal part of the life cycle, and they learn that by adults being open and honest. They use the right words — like "dying," "dead," "death," not "gone to sleep," "passed on," "lost." When pets die, there are funerals, services, burials. This gives a child a chance to say goodbye, to put some closure on the life but not the memory. Pets are not replaced immediately unless the child asks for another one. They must have time to grieve. Children learn a great deal about life from animals. They learn about survival, love and interaction. In the case of dogs, they learn unconditional love. They also learn that death is something over which they have no control. When that is handled in a healthy manner, other kinds of grieving are dealt with.

I can recall in my sickness telling my daughter, when her hamster died, "It's only a rodent; I'll get you another one!"

I shudder when I remember that episode. In retrospect, I should have known that my daughter, loving animals more than people, had things she needed to say.

Grieving is powerlessness. It needs the nurturing required for any other kind of pain. If children can truly learn that they have no power over life or death, they can learn that they are not responsible for divorce and separation, life-threatening illnesses, the family moving or other losses. Grieving children have an unquestionable need for compassion, mutual respect, listening and sharing. There is a need for holding, hugging and the freedom to express all feelings. There is a need for honest laughter — not ridicule. Above all, it is healthy to grieve in whatever way is appropriate for each person. Asking, "How can I help?" means possibly being told that you can't help.

What do normal children have that dysfunctional children do not?

1. Emotional security — a deep and abiding knowledge that they are loved and lovable.
2. They know they can accomplish anything to which they set their minds.
3. Success and failure are just words to them.
4. Wrong and right are feelings by which they can judge their own actions.
5. They do not fear other people, either their peers or "Big People."
6. They are not afraid that their significant people will stop loving them if they commit an irresponsible act or if their report cards aren't perfect.
7. They can show their feelings without fearing scorn or punishment.
8. They confirm themselves without destroying another person.
9. They can share themselves.
10. They love some kind of Higher Power.
11. They do the best they can and are satisfied with the results.
12. They do not beat up on themselves if they are not "perfect."

These, among many other characteristics and behaviors, form the basis of "normal." Adult Child Mourners can learn from such people, not by jealousy and envy but by treating their child within in like manner.

Doris tells me that she has come to terms with the childhood that never was by being the parent to her inner child. She now sees what she missed and can recreate a situation where she feels her little girl within is safe, secure and trusting in the adult Doris. How did Doris do that? By learning to laugh, have fun, keep it simple and be honest. She is the kind of parent to her little Doris that she couldn't be to her own children — the kind of mother her mother could not be to her.

Little Doris doesn't come first all the time. Life doesn't stand still for her. Instead, she is accepted by a very balanced down-to-earth, grown-up Doris. The woman has forgiven her parents for their behavior toward her and has begun to fulfill her own goals. She can say no now. She does not regress into, "My parents did this and that," ad nauseam. She is at peace with herself, so the manifold problems she still has achieve a less than prominent position in her life. She'll deal with them when she gets around to it. Her priorities are straight and she, with her inner child, knows the reality of living — and loving it.

7

What Counselors Need To Know

The treatment for Adult Child Mourners is unlike any other form of counseling. It is gentle, encouraging and takes a great deal of patience. Counselors are dealing with chronologically adult people, many of whom are extremely successful in their chosen careers and lifestyles. Emotionally, however, they are bereft children whose pain can manifest itself in many ways, from the tearful homemaker to the tantrums of the president of the company. If these people are still searching for what is not available, their private and personal lives will remain unmanageable.

From my own professional experience, I find it easier to work with the addict, even in relapse, than the Adult Child Mourner and Co-dependent. Most of the time I have to use restraint, being impatient for their recognition and recovery as only a recovering "one of their own" can be. In the search for perfection, particularly in relationships, I have to bite my tongue constantly. The "What, again?" wants to slither out. But by remembering how long it took me, I can control the impulse.

In treating Adult Child Mourners, it is essential to be conversant with the grieving process as described earlier. The most effective counselors are often Adult Child Mourners in their own recovery. It is extremely difficult otherwise to comprehend the enormity of a grief that occurred years prior to treatment. There is a tendency to give advice and say, "It's time to grow up."

It is crucial for counselors working in this field to fully comprehend the complicated predicament of the Adult Child Mourner. It is of equal importance for people who are struggling and confused to recognize the enormous amount of negative energy they are using to organize and accept their unhappy lifestyles. Too much struggle is attached to changing. Oftentimes it is a question of stopping behavior rather than seeking active "doing."

The most difficult advice to be followed by Adult Child Mourners is "Do nothing." Doing "something" had led to trauma, addiction, difficult relationships and pain.

Adult Child Mourners are told, "Don't react—act." Sometimes even that is too much. Consider the challenge of taking action on a situation about which there is complete ignorance. Remember, we are Adult Child Mourners. *We don't know what we are mourning.*

Certainly, some of the more advanced realize they are mourning their childhood. But what is a happy childhood? How do we know what we missed, having never had it?

All that Adult Child Mourners can recall is what they learned and observed growing up. Many times, without knowing why, they tried to escape from the unpleasantness. They didn't know whether it was right or wrong—had never heard of the word "dysfunction"—but just wanted to get away.

A small child recognizes the environment in which it lives as normal. Physical, emotional, mental and verbal abuse were constants for many children. It was their normal. To what could they compare their circumstances?

Being raised in an emotional void robs a child of the ability to feel. They cannot understand emotions because so many were stomped on during the formative years. Abuse is their frame of reference.

The conspiracy of silence and the resultant being invisible inhibit any form of expression. Children are lied to by the Big People who physically or verbally abuse one another and tell the children, "We're not angry." There are raging co-dependents who, while having their lights punched out, still tell the children, "we love one another."

I can remember as a small child being on my knees and praying that my parents would divorce. I was never granted that wish. In fact, I stayed in my own dysfunctional marriage for over 25 years until I suddenly realized I didn't have to do that anymore!

It is not only abusive behavior that robs children of their childhood. Being deprived can include taking on the role of being the parent's friend, confidante, buddy and companion. It is an unnatrual burden for a child to be expected to provide counseling for its parent. I did that to my youngest child. He is just learning today that he doesn't have to listen to everybody's woes. He is an Adult Child Mourner who, due to the grace of God, decided on therapy at the age of 22 to try to combat the poisonous influence with which he grew up.

In a dysfunctional family feelings are ephemeral. Being caught up in the swift mood changes, the child cannot grasp the terror of the moment. Nothing is balanced, nothing is stable.

In many cases crying was not permitted. In fact, very little emotional expression was allowed. Sadness was weak—you "just had to get over it," whatever "it" was—and get on with your life. Children who were raised in an emotional void had no concept of how to behave socially. They simply did not and do not as adults know what is acceptable and what is not. They have no knowledge of boundaries. The therapist's first understanding has to be that if Adult Child Mourners say they don't know how they feel—*they don't know.* Counseling has to start at zero, as if the patient were a newborn baby. Simple statements need to be repeated: "It wasn't my fault. There wasn't anything I could do about it. I was a little child."

Eileen's sister was murdered 25 years ago. Because of the conspiracy of silence at that time and since, she has just started to grieve. She is also just recognizing her own paternal issues. Eileen's counselor needs to know her stuff!

I recall interviewing an author recently on the subject of rape. I asked her about selecting a therapist. She referred to one of the earlier experiences she had by telling me that this therapist read up on her problem during the week and practiced on her in their session. That just won't do.

Again, counselors dealing with Adult Child Mourners must understand that when they ask "how do you feel?" about thus and such, the answer "I don't know" means the patient *does not know.* I recall an earlier therapist in my life screaming at me that I certainly *did* know what was wrong—I just wasn't telling her! She called me a slippery eel—just when she thought she got it I wriggled away. I thought I was crazy because I really didn't know and tortured myself trying to remember that which was securely locked in my subconscious.

The Inner Child

In addition, the counselor must be in touch with the needs of the inner child. The little one is deeply sad and frightened and wants comfort. Ask any Adult Child Mourner what they wanted from their parents when problems arose, and they will all say, "reassurance, comforting, telling me I was okay."

The child within and the Adult Child Mourner are both mourning. That has to be respected in the knowledge that recovery happens once trust is established.

How does a counselor establish an aura of trust with a person who doesn't know the meaning of the word? First comes listening to thoughts and feelings, especially the latter. I suggest that early sessions be conducted in the nature of quiet conversations—believe me, it gets noisier! If the counselor disagrees with comments made, trust has to be there before there is "significant" disagreement. Adult Child Mourners have to learn that agreeing to disagree is a part of normal behavior, but slowly does it. These people have just been born.

Touching

Healthy touch is crucial now, and I recommend great caution. There is a vast difference of opinion among therapists regarding hugging clients. My philosophy is that if we are helping people to deal with feelings, our own growth is an ongoing adventure. By growing, we can establish a certain knowledge as to whether a patient wants to be touched. There is a spiritual "knowing." If that natural instinct is not there yet, simply ask, "Do you like to be touched?"

A touch can be anything from a full body hug to a light tap on the hand. Never assume. If there is the slightest doubt as to how the person will react—ask.

Anger

Regarding reaction—anger is a large part of recovery. Adult Child Mourners have kept their anger under wraps for most of their lives. It is totally unacceptable to them. So many Adult Child Mourners end up by getting even instead of getting mad. This, of course, produces severe alienation because trust, if there was any, is broken. Anger is a very productive emotion if channelled correctly. At this stage of recovery it is essential that all judgments be suspended. If the counselor cannot deal with the Adult Child Mourner's anger, it is time to refer the person to a counselor who can. What is being dealt with here is a person who was never permitted to express emotions in a healthy way, if they even had any concept of what emotions were. So acceptance and common-sense feedback are essential at this point in treatment.

I was taught a most valuable lesson by a prisoner in a major penitentiary. He told me that it was possible, and indeed vital, for me "not to take anger personally."

The secret is to tell people who are expressing their anger that I am more than willing to listen to it and help them through the pain, but I will not own or be responsible for any of it. That works. It gives the patient the freedom to express the intensity as long as it is focused on the right situation. As I believe that anger is 50 percent physical, I frequently recommend going to a driving range and hitting golf balls, playing racquetball, running, shooting baskets, etc. I recommend these activities in addition to therapy and group counseling. It's true that some people hide behind the physical, but that's no reason why some outlet cannot be recommended for most patients.

The treatment of Adult Child Mourners is like no other. It is almost reparenting, but with adult respect for responsibility. Certainly Adult Child Mourners were powerless over whatever happened as children. Even if they had the wherewithal to make positive decisions, they couldn't carry them out. Now, as adults, they can. A most important factor in recovery is for the Adult Child Mourners to know that they don't have to stay Adult Child Mourners and that their change will be their decision. You, as the counselor, will be there to help them achieve that goal, though the work will definitely be theirs.

Self-Help Groups

Another point of concern is the pain experienced as the layers of denial are lifted. The counselor must be reasonably available in the early stages of recovery because the levels lift dramatically. It is of extreme importance that the patient is introduced to an appropriate self-help group or placed in a therapy group.

My preference is for these recovering people to be in therapy groups of their own sex. I have run both and find that the depth of honesty is much more profound in a "same sex" group.

I have discovered that, even in the serious quest for recovery, the Adult Child Mourner's behavior will be very different in the presence of the opposite sex. It is indefinable but it is present, almost as if there is a hidden tape of "how we should be" in such circumstances. It is a proven fact that men can see right through men and women through women. There seems to be an atmosphere of competition in mixed groups that is totally absent in same sex groups. As a result, more is observed more quickly and the bonding is stronger. In the mixed groups there is a tendency to "let the men share first." In this way the purpose is lost. Adult Child Mourner groups are not designed to deal with problems with the opposite sex —

there are special groups for that. These Adult Child Mourner groups are to learn about one's self and the long-hidden repressed beauty therein. They are to focus on self-confidence, recognition of personal potential, communications, spirituality and growth.

Relaxation Techniques

Counselors need to have a working knowledge of relaxation techniques. In order to meet and encourage the child within, living as it does in the subconsciouis mind, relaxation exercises and guided imagery are important. In order to relax, a person has to trust. Therefore it helps to explain what relaxation is. My definition is "a stress-free mind and body." Of course, it is necessary to explain that this is not a permanent state of mind. Some stress at some time is inevitable. Music is helpful. The introduction to the exercise must emphasize the fact that group members are in control of their lives during relaxation. Remember, we are dealing with low-trust people here. People have been exposed to the entertainment industry's idea of hypnosis, where people behave like washing machines or ducks or whatever the performer selects to make them look foolish and the entertainer look good. Participants in relaxation exercises need to be reassured that the facilitator is not a brainwasher.

It is preferable to keep relaxation exercises simple. New Age music is an enhancement to this work. It is important that facilitators have either taken some training in this module or use responsibly taped cassettes. The exercise should not be longer than 15 minutes, concentrating on nurturing the child within.

I toyed with the idea of writing several fantasy journeys in this book. However, I believe it is crucial for counselors to have their own full training in this area, since it is working with people's subconscious minds. Hypnotherapy and relaxation training are readily available to most counselors. This is not a situation in which one can experiment in the hope that it will work by itself. No practitioner can be sure of how people will react to this. Some people simply cannot relax or they get in touch with something from the past that frightens them, so responsible knowledge is required in this treatment module.

One of the most important things the counselor needs to know is how to raise children in a positive, loving, common-sense fashion. That's what you'll be introducing to Adult Child Mourners. You'll be dealing with the "shoulds," the "ought tos," the "if onlys." My response to all those things is, "Who wrote the rules?"

Then we go into action with, "Let's write our own rules and create our own normal." Excitement!

As stated in the miraculous Twelve-Step Program: "There is no easier, softer way." In this instance the levels of grieving are essential. Giving oneself permission to feel and learn to forgive (not condone) is a necessary process.

Depending on the personality of the individual Adult Child Mourner, any level of grieving can come at any given time. All, however, will be experienced. It is a question of being de-educated and re-educated, de-parented and re-parented. Treatment is important. The Adult Child Mourner has to be helped to achieve enough self-worth to understand that treatment is a gift, not a punishment.

The main recovery process takes place when Adult Child Mourners make a commitment to themselves to enter treatment for their own improved mental health. This decision opens the way for so much more. Levels of denial are lifted — a frightening but essential aspect of recovery. You can't heal what you don't know. *Warning — do not attempt to do this alone!* Remember, you're dealing with your subconscious memories. We need objective, compassionate people to help us through this painful but inevitably rewarding ordeal.

To discover the healing process, the Adult Child Mourner has to learn to nurture the child within. This is the way we learn the true essence of universal and unconditional love.

It is simple. We, as adults, know that we would not allow anyone to harm our children or any child we know. Therefore, we have to change our thinking from being annoyed at the antics of the child within to supporting that child. Here the inspiration is a powerful tool. Take your child to the zoo, to the store to buy some new clothes, to Disney World, to buy a toy — whatever would please you that you did not have.

The bottom line is understanding that what we knew as normal does not have to remain as our new normal. We can create our own normal. Who made the rules, anyway?

I have learned that what happened to me as a child was unconscionable. I did not know as a child what a happy childhood was. I do know what it is as a 56-year-old woman. This is not my second childhood — it's my first and I like it! What I have learned to do is stop the blaming and start being responsible for my own happiness. The grieving process turns to the healing process when we know we do not have to accept the package that was handed to us.

In your new awareness, start as you mean to continue. Affirmations are essential. Realize that it takes time, that you and your Higher Power can work on that schedule. Remember that laughter is a restorative tool. Laughing *with* yourself, not *at* yourself, is a primary goal. Being in recovery means allowing yourself to be silly at times, to giggle uncontrollably, to have special time with yourself, bubble baths, toys and *fun, fun, fun.* Yes, gentlemen, bubble baths for you too!!!

8

Recovery

Part I: Treatment Options And Choosing A Counselor

This chapter is divided into Parts I and II. The first part addresses what counselors need to know, including how to choose a counselor. Part II is my own recovery process.

What does that word — recovery — mean? People who do not understand the problems of Adult Child Mourners have no concept of the long-term recovery process. It is important for Adult Child Mourners to be aware of "People, Places and Things" early on in their commitment to treatment. A recovering alcoholic may not find compassion for his situation as an Adult Child Mourner among the fellowship of Alcoholics Anonymous. There is much denial in the membership because the truth is hard to face. Pain, feelings of disloyalty or simple blackouts contribute to this denial.

If the Adult Child Mourner is also an addict, priorities have to be set as to which condition is causing the most difficulty. It does seem to be wise to work with the primary problem for a year or so before tackling the secondary — if it can wait. I believe that when a person is in treatment for any compulsive behavior, adult child issues must be addressed in order to assess the priority need. This decision requires the objective viewpoint of a mental health practitioner well-versed in addictions and adult child treatments.

Whatever treatment is recommended, it is important to support that treatment by attending the relevant 12-Step Program. Local AA, Al-Anon, Overeaters Anonymous or other support groups will provide information on what a 12-Step Program is — important knowledge for counselors to have in their referral documents.

Treatment Modalities

There are several available options for treatment for Adult Child Mourners:

- Five-day outpatient
- 5½-day inpatient facility
- 12-day inpatient
- 28-day inpatient facility
- Intensive outpatient facility

Inpatient treatment is designed to give adult children an opportunity to recognize the malfunctions in the family of origin, examine them on a deep, intensive level and start the processes of growth and change. Expression of emotions, together with informative didactic presentations, encourage patients to begin the understanding that is a prerequisite to recovery. Contrary to the analytical discipline of the past, it is not necessary to delve into every corner of the childhood years. Rather it is essential to look at the blocks of today and seek some knowledge of what went before to recognize the connections. It is valuable to examine the patients' relationships with their parents and what they observed between the parents. After all, that's the frame of reference from which emanates all intimacy.

Family sculpting vividly portrays the atmosphere of the childhood. The patient can frequently see and feel what went on in their family of origin even though up to that point the memory may have been blocked.

Many professionals advocate the five-day outpatient program. The participants attend five full days and return to their homes at night. This addresses the need to maintain their family without too much disruption and reduces the guilt that many Adult Child Mourners have with real or imagined abandonment issues. Having been through inpatient treatment myself, I couldn't conceive going home every night as if nothing more than a working day had happened. If nothing else, I was delighted at being unable to use a telephone for five full days!

For the vast majority of people, 5½ days of treatment is enough information for them to be working on for another three years. Some need more help and enter a 12- or 28-day program. Some Adult Child Mourners may have to start with the five-day program and then try another later. Adult Child Mourners have different depths of anguish.

Re-entry is a very clear problem. After five days of intensive therapy in a womblike environment, entering the birth canal can be traumatic. This process seems to affect people in one of three ways:

1. They float out on a pink cloud.
2. They crawl out under a black cloud.
3. Nothing penetrated the shell.

My feelings on re-entry from all programs, regardless of time or intensity, have always been very strong. Appropriate support at this time is vital.

I have very definite standards for admission to treatment. I will not recommend that any person enter treatment for adult child grief or any other adult child/co-dependency issue, without having been involved with at least one of the following:

1. Private therapy for at least six months with a counselor familiar with adult child issues, co-dependency and grief.

2. Women's or men's therapy groups for at least six months with a facilitator knowledgeable in adult child, co-dependency and grief issues. This also will serve as an aftercare group.

3. Attend two meetings of a 12-Step program per week for at least six months.

4. If not in a group, set up an aftercare group *before* entering the program. This often can be done by asking the treatment program for suggestions.

5. If asking the treatment program is not practical because it's a distance away, ask members of local ACoA or ACoDP meetings for information. (Of course, you will have to ask individuals before or after the meeting.)

When looking for an appropriate treatment facility, remember to ask questions. In fact, knowing Adult Child Mourners as I do, I suggest you write a list of questions before you call and read them off. If you don't get any answers, call another facility. Now, they aren't going to tell you their entire program — that would be foolish and inappropriate. Assess that the questions are reasonable (You can do that, can't you?) and ask them. If you don't have any questions, that's okay too. I didn't — I just love surprises!

The Holistic Approach

Because of the intricacies of an Adult Child Mourner's childhood, developing a therapeutic approach to treatment has been somewhat difficult. Many times a dual diagnosis is overlooked due to the complex nature of the dysfunction, and frequently only one diagnosed condition is treated, mainly that of depression.

Unless all aspects of negative projection are erased, recovery is impossible. Positive attitudes are essential. This requires a happy, confident treatment team. The four areas to be addressed in treatment are: mental, physical, emotional and spiritual. The whole person came from a dysfunctional family — the whole person has to be involved in recovery. Eliminating any one of these areas detracts from total recovery.

What is it that Adult Child Mourners recognize clearly?

1. That they are indeed survivors.
2. That they have personality problems such as perfectionism, inability to express anger and difficulty with relationships and intimacy.
3. That they have problems with physical pain as a result of severe tension and stress.
4. That they don't know where to fit in.

An inpatient program has to address the implications of the complicated thinking of adult children. These emotional persons seem to be within the restrictions and imprisonment of total helplessness at times. They are vulnerable when exposed to extreme behaviors from others and are highly influenced by people close to them. There are always the dangers of constant approval-seeking and excessive co-dependency with another person or group. Therefore, the program has to address self-esteem, the spirituality of self-caring (including constructive humor), the philosophy of the 12-Step program (which incorporates literature, sponsorship, attendance at meetings and sharing) and the ability to say "no" without explanations as and when choice decrees it.

It is essential for Adult Child Mourners to learn how to play and how to channel their anger, sadness and grief positively. Therefore, it is essential for all counselors, all faculty, all staff to be conscious of the workings of the adult child's mind plus the grief process and to be flexible in their approach. Certainly there is a basic instruction and philosophy, and it is important for therapists and counselors to be sufficiently aware of their own adult child issues in dealing with their patients. They can then vary responses to people and understand that, although the program is set, there are exceptions at times. Things can be changed in the moment of priority need.

What we are looking at here is a recovery program, a solution. The first two days in treatment will deal with the problem. Then "life after survival" options have to be made available for people so that when they leave the facility they have not only hope, but actual instructions and directions to further treatment.

Because of the certain knowledge that young children internalize rather than verbalize, it is unnecessary to examine
patients' character defects in depth. It is important to recognize them. Suffice it to say that they are there as means of
survival. These survival skills, in fact, could be defined as
destructive at times, especially if they include addictions. Part
of the treatment process is to take those very survival skills
and turn them around to produce positive action. An example
is that somebody who is excessively willful and stubborn to
their own detriment can be shown how that consistency can
be turned around to be extremely productive in terms of their
career, profession, lifestyle, relationship, etc.

Clarity is essential in early treatment. There has been too
much secrecy in childhood, and clear expression has to be a
high priority. This includes explaining that adult child inpatient treatment in no way is designed to blame parents. Once
the denial is broken, tremendous rage and anger need to be
dealt with. The timing has to be right to present the fact that
the perpetrators were ill themselves. Although the behavior is
not condoned, there are ways of letting go. It is important for
counselors to be able to express just how this forgiveness can
take place without the loss of dignity or a feeling of "giving
in." If the parents are still living, then attention has to be paid
to what is within the control of the Adult Child Mourner and
what is not. It is important to keep the focus on recovery and
loosening the chains of the past.

In the holistic approach it is important for people to recognize the spirit within in terms of relaxation, music and touch.
The Higher Power is directly connected to the person within,
and attention has to be paid to that grief-stricken, suffering
child encased in the adult body. One of the hazards in this
which has to be avoided at all costs is that when the child
within is recognized, he or she becomes a total brat. This is
not the idea of this treatment, which is basically reparenting:
learning to use firmness and confrontation very, very gently.
The idea is to teach the patient to become the parent of the
suffering child within and to treat that child in a way they
would like to have been treated. However, it has to remain
clear to staff members that very many times these people

don't know how they would like to have been treated. They only know that they wanted "it" stopped.

For a person who was raised in an emotional void, there is no frame of reference whatsoever. Emotions were either not expressed or overexpressed. Either way, nothing was accomplished — just invisibility for the victimized child. Therefore, basic emotions and their expression have to be taught. This can be done by psychodrama, writing, drawing, etc. It is an essential part of recovery that people express themselves in whichever way is the most suitable for them. Some people are more articulate than others, more verbal. Some people see things. They have visualizations. Other people can touch, listen or write. It is essential in this program that we use the tool with which the person is most comfortable. It is important to see which particular strength each person has and utilize that in the individual assignments given to them. A basic introduction to neurolinguistics would be helpful in training.

In addition to group, where childhood issues will be discussed and psychodrama will take place, one-on-one counseling is important. It should be both written into the program and made available at times of breakthroughs which may well happen. It is important for staff members to be on hand at most times — to counsel, not just count heads.

As it is a holistic program, obviously the physical has to be considered. I strongly suggest that an exercise instructor be retained to produce an aerobic program to really connect mind, body and spirit. In addition to this, of course, it is of extreme importance to provide a healthy, appropriate diet.

Another aspect to be strongly addressed in treatment is the "no talk" rule — the inordinate fear of recognition. People need not only recovery to be made part of the solution, but a sense of pride in being an adult child who survived and is now going on to bigger and better things.

One of the training aspects is for people to be able to open that part of the potential that is frequently ignored: creativity. Creativity is important in the recovery process, not in terms of sewing, cooking and painting, but rather creativity from within. It grows from expressing oneself, sharing, listening, caring about other people and relating to other people.

People get well without realizing it. Recovery is subjective, so feedback is essential. Learning to concentrate on things that can be changed and letting go of those that cannot is the essence of spirituality.

The two biggest problems in treatment are control issues and problems with intimacy. It's important that people give others in their group permission to express what they feel about those particular issues that they see or feel coming from one another.

The staffing of this community has to be from professionals who are empathetic to the conditions of co-dependency, grieving and adult children. In addition, their training must be continuous. Of course, they have to have personally experienced an inpatient five-day program whether they are Adult Child Mourners or not.

Staff support groups are essential, as this therapeutic model can be emotionally exhausting to the facilitator. My recommendation is that the staff have at least two daily 20-minute relaxation periods of meditation or guided imagery. One period can be on their own and one be facilitated by a hypnotherapist or other professional.

The emotional, physical, spiritual and mental health of the staff is just as important as that of the patients.

Choosing The Counselor

How do you select the right counselor? By taking a risk. Adult Child Mourners have difficulty in so doing.

1. *Ask,* "Are you familiar with the Adult Child Syndrome and Grief?"
2. Are they sitting behind a desk? If so, get out!
3. Do you feel comfortable with them? This is a big one! Adult Child Mourners think they *should* give people the benefit of the doubt. There is time enough to feel uncomfortable when the layers of denial are lifted. It is the counselor's responsibility to make you feel comfortable at the first session. Sometimes the chemistry just isn't right. *You can change your mind!* You don't

have to be with someone in conflict. *You are allowed to feel comfortable.*
4. People do outgrow their therapists. Don't stay in a situation where you feel you are the counselor. Adult Child Mourners "don't want to hurt anyone's feelings." (Only their own.)
5. Ask members of your 12-Step program if they know of any counselors who have proven effective. Remember that one person's fish is another's poison, but it is a start as to who is in the field.
6. Is it "Dr. so-and-so" or first-name basis? With which are you more comfortable?
7. *Remember, doctors and therapists are not gods.*
8. Make a list at the consultation if you can't rely on your memory.
9. *Pray a lot.*

Part II: My Own Recovery Process

I had made many attempts to break the invisible chain that kept me attached to unrewarding situations. Personally and professionally I was not fulfilling my potential. I was in therapy, attending ACoA meetings, yet something was missing. Some people were coming to meetings looking "different." They talked of major breakthroughs and the inpatient facility that helped them in 5½ days. I thought, "Impossible." I listened carefully. I checked it out and registered. Of course, I allowed myself to select a session nine months ahead, to be sure.

I entered the Caron Family Treatment Center for Adult Children because I had issues of grief which I had not fully recognized. When I walked in there, I saw young counselors running around who probably were wearing diapers when I first started. I looked at them and I thought "Right! They're going to tell *me?*" Big whoop! That was my attitude. I went in 100 percent professional person and radio personality, and I thought, "I'm not going to let them know who I am because I don't want to be treated any differently."

Peter, my counselor, called me into the office and said, "Why aren't you telling anybody who you are?"

I said, "Because I don't want to be treated any differently. I want to be treated like everybody else. I just want to get well, Peter."

He said, "Well, you're not telling anyone what you do for a living. People will ask you and you'll say 'I work.' "

I said, "I do work."

"You just say, 'I work with people.' "

"I do work with people."

"Why don't you tell them?"

"If they know who I am, I know they're going to be different."

"You know what I think it is, Yvonne? I think you're afraid they won't know who you are."

I thought, "Bingo!" He hit the nail right on the head. I was in that place for half an hour and I had it. Boom! Right in the face. From then on it was down and then up. It was wonderful and very scary. These people knew what was required. Even the sculpting they did with me was exactly what I needed.

The program dealt with a lot of co-dependency issues that I use today, because I became my mother's mother at the age of nine and always took care of everybody. Everyone else was much more important than me. It happened in treatment, too. I'd sit and wait for everybody else to talk. I didn't want to take up too much time. Boy, is that control! "Look at me! Look at me!! I'm not going to take up too much time."

So they'd ask, "What's the matter, Yvonne?" I got everything I wanted. All the attention I wanted. Finally, though, they saw through that. They'd say, "Oh God. Here comes the therapist again. When's the child coming out?"

What do we do when we don't deal with grief? We make ourselves ill. We've been told that. All the medical associations all over the world say, "Internalized stress can cause illness." We see it constantly.

Recovery from the grieving process really has to do with very simple statements like this: "It wasn't my fault. There wasn't anything that I could do about this. I was a little child."

I had to look at these things and let go by looking at the control issue. It sometimes meant saying the serenity prayer three or four times an hour and really listening to it. That is pure logic. I'm not a logical woman, but that serenity prayer is the most important piece of logic in my life. I had to say it slowly and really listen to it. There are things over which I had no control as a child. As an adult I do.

One of the ways I dealt with rage as an adult is that I looked at it with the feelings of a child. What would I do if I had that little child right in front of me now? I do an exercise sometimes when I teach a graduate course in this. I ask people to look at a little child sitting on the curb crying. What would you do with that child? They come up with all kinds of things they would do to comfort that child and try to make it feel secure. There's no reason why I couldn't do that to my child within.

In the grieving process, when it applies to Adult Child Mourners, it is not the adult who is grieving. It's the child. The vast majority of people who really begin to identify their pain realize that it started about the age of six. That seems to be a real common denominator. I got in my head what a little child of six would do in such dire circumstances and what I could do to help that child. What did that child need? I closed my eyes and just allowed my pen to run on the paper and write everything that came through my mind. I know what that child within me still needs because she's still breathing. I hadn't recognized I was stuck in the pain of the past. I now know that the little child was confused, unhappy and didn't know who she could turn to. All I know is there was a lot of pain.

Rage and helplessness. They are synonymous. What's in the middle of those two things? Control. When I was at Caron, that's what they dealt with. That's what I mean about it being subtle. When I went in, they said, "What do you want to deal with?"

I said, "Problems of intimacy."

"What else?"

"That's all."

"Fine."

When I got the treatment sheet, it said, "We want you to deal with your control of yourself and others and the amount of control."

I roared, "That's not what I'm here for."

Peter said, "See — *you're doing it now.*"
"*I wanted to deal with what I wanted to deal with.*"
Being in the five-day program allowed me to do things I
hadn't done for years. I cried. I yelled. I played. I was silly. I
told of my pain. I was listened to instead of being the constant
listener. I became part of the lives of other people who wanted
to recover. I found a kind of love I had never known before.
They call it unconditional.

On leaving Caron, I entered aftercare one night a week.
Through rain, hail, stormy nights, snow, slush — like the Post
Office, I never missed. Treatment had opened up so many
black holes. I needed this.

After about seven months I entered another facility, this
time for four days. I went to a place called the Shalom Mountain to a man called Dr. Jerry Judd. He is about 70 now. He
looks like Moses. As soon as he saw me, he said, "Why have
you taken so long to come to the mountain?"

I thought "Oops. He's been floating around and watching
me."

I didn't have an answer to that. I thought I was going on a
retreat. You know how people go around all quiet and holy on
retreats. Not there! He was trained in Esalen and into primal
scream and all that kind of thing. My primal scream was a
squeak and that was an effort. I could listen to everybody else
scream their guts out, but not me. (When I did that at Caron,
Peter said, "I think you can do a little bit better than that.")

There were about 14 of us in the group. Dr. Judd dealt with
each one of us individually. Everybody sat around on this huge
mattress thing. When he was working with us, we wore a
blindfold so there was no distraction at all. There was a whole
lot of love. It was scary at first but basically just a beautiful
experience. I had never been loved like that before. I never
had a relationship that wasn't conditional. When it was my turn,
he just held me, rocked me and said, "Was this familiar?"

I said, "No. This never happened to me before. I never
remember my parents ever saying, 'I love you' or anything of
that nature." I had forgotten Mrs. Harrison.

He said to me, "What do you want to deal with?"

I said, "I have no idea. I just turned it over this morning and whatever comes out, comes out."

What came out were my experiences in the war, being in the blitz and being sent away. I screamed that out in a way I never thought I could. It was fascinating for me because when I was finished, nobody was shocked. Nobody was horrified. They were loving and caring. I couldn't believe that these people were that way with me because, after all, I didn't deserve that. I wasn't worthy.

Dr. Judd maintains that little children make powerful decisions in order to survive. They're not good ones, but they make them. He said, "What decisions did you make when you were six, Yvonne?"

The first one out of my mouth was, "I was never going to let anyone love me." I didn't. Let me tell you how I did it because maybe you can relate to this.

I didn't let anyone love me because I loved them. I did for them. I gave for them. They didn't have time to get in. I wasn't going to learn it anyway. People would say to me, "Let me do something for you." "No. No. No."

I was a recovering martyr, too. I could do everything like a good co-dependent. I think it's wonderful that they gave us a name, don't you? We used to be enablers. Now we're co-dependent. I like that. It gives me a sense of pride!

Dr. Judd said to me, "That's not enough. There's something else."

I said, "I think that's enough. I had screwy relationships up until recently. I think that's enough."

He said, "No. There's something else."

So he started talking about the war. Guns, bombs, planes and then said the one thing that can drive me crazy. "What we need is another war."

I lost it. I screamed and ranted and raved.

He said, "What was it? What was the decision?"

The decision, when I was eight, was that I wanted to die. I just wanted to die. I set about doing that. I didn't eat. I didn't sleep. I didn't talk. Nothing. This is when I was evacuated. I was sent back to London because I just couldn't handle it. I have Post-Traumatic Stress Disorder from those days. It's not as bad as it used to be because I dealt with that on the mountain.

One miracle that happened when I went home helped me realize there was a change in me. I didn't say to my son Daniel right away, "You've got to take this course!" As soon as I came out of Caron I was going to "put my children in." My children, however, have minds of their own. I can't imagine where they got that from!

I was very quiet after my work at Shalom Mountain, and I realized I had literally done something I had never given myself permission to do. That was to scream out the rage. I have a tape of that. When I first came out, I would listen to the tape. I used to turn the volume down because I couldn't stand the screams. Now I have it on full blast because I have the right.

One astounding result of this was that I came home, went to bed that night and about 3:00 o'clock in the morning became deadly ill. I thought I was dying. That went on for a couple of days. I couldn't move because I was so ill. A friend of mine who had been at Caron called and said, "You sound awful. What's the matter?"

I told him what had happened and he said, "Yvonne, you're detoxing."

I said, "I haven't touched anything for years."

He said, "All that suppression, all that pain, agony and hell from your childhood has now been released and it's coming out through your pores."

One of the things that Dr. Judd had said to me when I told him of my two childhood decisions was, "Now I have to help you reverse those decisions."

In those three days when I literally thought I was dying, I was reversing those decisions. Miracles do happen in this program. It takes courage to face the pain, but pain is the great healer. You're not looking to hurt yourself. You're looking to *unhurt* yourself. You've got to go through the valley. You have to go through the reasons why your life was not the way you wanted it to be. Maybe it's still not the way you wanted it to be. It's still all caught up in that pain of childhood that we have not dealt with.

One of the most common reasons I hear to avoid that pain is that, "My parents couldn't help it. My childhood wasn't so bad."

No, my childhood wasn't *so* bad. It was worse than bad. When I stopped minimizing that, I felt I had the right to get rid of that pain. I could get rid of that rage and still keep the memory of my mother intact with a lot of love. That's when I started to get healthy.

It's frightening to say that: "You've got to face the pain." Why do you think they say "no pain, no gain"? It's real. I don't care how many times people come up with all kinds of different ways of circumventing and running around this pain. I looked it right in the eye. I recognized my enemy and made it my friend. That's how it works. If you keep running away from it, it is going to keep chasing you.

Recovery from this is not about blame. It is about truly facing the fact that things done in my childhood were unconscionable. I went through pain that small children should never, ever, ever have to experience.

Max

When Max was a little boy he lived in an atmosphere of coldness except for the whippings he received. He lived in the pain of the awful relationship between his parents and their adoring of his brother and sister. And he wet the bed. It was out of his control. When he awoke every morning, he would be terrified. His family humiliated him because of his problem — there was no sensitivity, no compassion. He was a nuisance. His mother had had a bad delivery when he was born, and that was his fault, too. So he became enuretic and petrified. Something froze in him.

One day Max woke up and was so afraid that he set fire to his mattress. I asked him what happened. Maybe one day we'll find out what his family did at that time. For now, it's a total blackout.

Max is surviving. He is recovering and will do well. When he recalls this incident in full — and he will — he will handle it.

I survived. Now I have to live. When I live, I live with the grief. It becomes recovery. It becomes healing. It gets to a point that when I deal with whatever particular problem I have here, it becomes exciting. I get some pain and I think, "Wow! Something new is happening here." I can recognize it now without it getting to the acutely painful stage. In the past it used to terrify me. It's exciting now.

The bottom line of it all is that I had to learn to love myself enough to take the risk to change. I really do believe that I have to love myself before I can love someone else. Although having someone healthy to love me does help. I said before that I am not a logical woman. I'm not a mathematician by any stretch of the imagination. An interesting thing happened on my geometry exam when I was 15. My math teacher said, "You would do well to rely on your theorems rather than your womanly intuition."

That was 40 years ago, but I'll never forget that woman. I'm not logical, but even I know I can't give away what I don't have. It is not selfish to love myself. It is self-caring. It is important to take care of myself so I can spread whatever it is that I want to spread among people I love. I had to go through this process.

If you find yourself being very angry or you get sad, take it somewhere. Don't avoid the issue. Go to a therapist. Go to a counselor. Go to a group. Talk it through. *You have the right.*

I encourage you to read the books of Elisabeth Kubler-Ross. She's not talking to Adult Child Mourners, and yet she is. If you take out the word cancer, liver malfunction or whatever it is that she's talking about and you put childhood co-dependency and grief in there, what she writes makes just as much sense.

There is one other thing I want you to recognize because a lot of people don't and it is a big healer — *humor.* Allow yourself to have fun. I had to learn at Caron how to have fun. I didn't know how to do that. I always had to be so damn responsible. That always comes from all these issues. So you have to learn to lighten up a little bit.

Maybe in recovery you're going to have to take one tiny little step at a time. That's okay. Sometimes you take two steps forward and three steps back. Then there's the time when you take three steps forward and two steps back. You gain. You're always going to gain. As they say in AA, "AA spoils your drinking." "Recovery spoils your relapse," in this particular area. The more you deal with the grief, the more you learn to let go of the pain and understand that grieving is a process. It's a way of life. You're not going to get through life without grief.

Dr. Judd worked in the peace movement and one of the things he said to me when I was doing the screaming bit was, "We do a lot of work in the peace movement but your screams have a certain authenticity. You need to take them somewhere for world peace."

I said, "Oh God. I really just want to go home and eat ice cream, but I'm not supposed to do that either."

Wouldn't you know that three weeks after I came out of treatment, I was called to the United Nations? I called him and said, "What did you do?"

He said, "Nothing. I didn't do anything."

I realized that I was working through this exactly the way I was supposed to do. I had turned around those two decisions I made as a child. One result was that my whole method of counseling changed. I began to guide my clients to look at those decisions that we all made, to survive this grief and come through to be survivors, then to turn it around to have this miraculous life after survival — *one day at a time*. The beauty of it is that I can feel lousy today and that's okay. I don't have to be up all the time. When I feel that I am no longer grieving and dealing with issues but say, "I happen to feel lousy today," then I know that's recovery.

So that's the treatment bit for me. What else did I do? Whatever it takes. This part is where the freedom I learned so well from the teachings of Dr. Viktor Frankl takes form. This part is where "whatever it takes" enhances my recovery.

There are some very talented ethical people in the parapsychology field whose help has been essential in my life, growth and recovery. As a holistic health believer, I endorse mind, body and spirit as the only path to recovery. And I do believe in total recovery from this particular condition.

For some years I have been consulting with specialists who

have taught me how to use my mind and enhance my spirituality. When I have a physical problem, I consult a doctor. At the same time I visit with a hypnotherapist, a psychic counselor and a one-brain integrationist. The first person taught me how to relax and look within to help nurture the child. The second taught me where I was putting my negative stress and why I was stuck in my recovery at that particular time. Having learned from these two women what I had to deal with and confront, I then met with the body energy. For a long time I have stated that people do not listen to the messages their bodies send and that's why there is so much sickness. I did not realize that there were people who actually worked with these messages.

My most recent experiences deserve attention. The truth in my life is that my Higher Power works in wondrous ways — truly marvelous, exciting ways. I often find myself failing to listen to my body messages, mainly because as a woman I consider myself invincible. So I tend to delay things somewhat. However, Higher Power catches up with all of us if we ignore things. Part of my procrastination is putting off the recognition that any of these physical things are connected with my adult child grieving issues. *Wrong!*

Not long ago, as a gracious concession to the gynecologist, I had a mammogram. I was recalled. I had another mammogram to my chagrin. (In other words, my control took a beating.) There was "something nebulous" on the X-ray, necessitating a visit to a specialist. I immediately called Mary, the psychic counselor and one-brain integrationist.

One outcome of my time with Mary was realizing that I had not entirely let go of my children to let them grow and make their own problems which required their own solutions. I recognized I was still doing that with one daughter. Adult Child Mourners have a terrible time with feeling guilty about parenting and giving what they never had. The second situation was due to a very peculiar happening. After having had pierced ears for some 32 years, my earrings started falling out. I lost over a dozen pairs of earrings. Mary informed me that I was interfering in a major meridian flow and, more to the point, I wasn't listening! I said, "I can't understand why this is happening. I've never been so happy in my life. I have a healthy partner in life who loves me unconditionally — what else? Until I met him, I only trusted two men and I gave birth to them both!"

Mary's response was, "Well, you controlled both of them."

All right, Mary!

From there I went directly to Barbara Rose. The first thing she does each time is to balance me, and at this session didn't she start talking about meridians? She hadn't done that before. She cleared them and then said something was blocked.

"Try my ears," I said.

Right on! She continued to work on my emotional blocks, all of which made sense. Then she asked me to relax, to visualize colors and shapes, and then she said, "What do you see?"

What I saw was the profile of a beautiful woman in her 30s wearing a cloche hat. I started to talk about this woman and suddenly said, "Oh my God, it's my mother."

She was about 30 when I was born.

Barbara said, "It's time for forgiveness. Tell her you forgive her. She wants to know what you didn't have. What she didn't give you."

I responded, "My childhood."

Barbara said, "She wants you to forgive her; she wants to help you now. Ask her to forgive you, too."

The conversation was more in depth and I spoke with my mother, reaching that place of security I never expected to achieve.

Barbara then told me that my mother would be with me for the next three months to help me through whatever I needed, and that I should call her by her given name.

In those three hours I was shown the journey I had to take — forgiveness and patience. This was to be done in my way, with humor and fun, self-acceptance and love. There was much more, not necessarily revelant to this book but fascinating to my personal growth. One of the most important aspects of this involvement was that I was shown how to end this book. I am very grateful for that.

In an earlier chapter I did a chart with four significant
people who influenced my early years. Here's the chart today
in my recovery:

Jane. A feisty, highly intelligent, creative, warm and loving
woman. She started me on my most exciting journey as a
lecturer. Jane has helped me fulfill in my career the premoni-
tion Dr. Alex had regarding me. She argues with me lovingly,
points out character defects and more character assets. She
has helped in presentations, marketing, appearance — she is
a mentor. Jane is intimidated by no one, especially me. She
took me to Bill W.'s grave and taught me humility. She is
reality. She made me face it, too. I watch her and I learn.

Daniel. My youngest child — funny, creative, deep, pain-
fully honest with me, outrageous, satirical. He probably knows
me better than anyone. He can be arrogant, outspoken, insecure, sad. I've watched him grow in awe. Incredibly artistically
talented, he is at the point of refusing to accept "anything
less." He has taught me wisdom and accepts me as I am. Now
he has to detach and go his way. I watch in gratitude and love.

Doris. A woman of great depth and human loyalty and
love. She knows *all,* is supportive and shows me total acceptance and unconditional love. When I "mess up" I'm on the
phone immediately. Her rigorous honesty has caused me to
feel homicidal at times, but she has this uncanny knack of
being right most of the time! She knows my potential better
than she knows her own and is not backward in coming
forward if I'm out of line. When I broke my leg, she bought
me bubbles to blow.

John. My gift from God. All my trusted friends who have
watched and seen me grow through one dysfunction after
another rejoice with me at having this man in my life. Know
that this is a miracle. He teaches me to laugh, to play, to be
silly. He welcomes my child to come out and play. He has
helped heal many childhood horrors simply by saying, "I think
that's enough now." He taught me to tend to business and find
structure in my finances. He is supportive and accepts me
totally as I am. He stays when bad things happen to me. He
endured my sabotage at the beginning of the relationship. He

is *not* an adult child; *he is normal.* I'm getting there. As well as my significant other partner, he is my most beloved friend.

Just recently I read a book that affected me deeply — Roseanne Barr's *Roseanne.* She wrote to her children but what impressed me most was that she wrote that book completely as she wanted to. She is a brilliant woman, and she gave herself the freedom to express herself and her life exactly as it was and is. That's what I intend to do. It was invigorating to read it. I learned a lot.

That's my recovery — I love it, pain and all! From pain came the beauty I live today, to which I have a right. And so do you.

9

No New Beginnings Without Endings

As a grief counselor I learned about death, dying and separation. I learned that until I recognized the inevitability of my own death, I could not live a fulfilled life. It has taken many years, but I do have that total acceptance today. I'm not interested in "pettiness," in gossip, in revenge. I don't care who's sleeping with whom. I only react when people preach against others that which they are doing in secret. I don't do hypocrisy. In my sickness I used to, but not now. The rigorous honesty has taken root.

What did I have to end?

Being deadly serious — about everything.
Blaming my parents for everything.
Feeling shame.
Hiding behind my dysfunctional non-childhood.
Perfectionism.

117

Being totally responsible for everything and everybody —
    their feelings, their lives.
Workaholism to hide the pain.
High expectations of others.
Looking-good family.
Being involved with people emotionally unavailable to me.
Rigid viewpoints.
Low self-esteem.
Fear of intimacy.
Martyrdom.
Wanting to control everybody in my life.
Being out of control of my own life.
Wanting what I *thought* I wanted.
Being dishonest under the guise of denial.
Feeling jealous of others' recognitions and advancement.
Being financially helpless.
Competitiveness.
Inferiority complex.
Hating my appearance.

The list is endless. It lasted many years. I adopted the behaviors to which I was exposed growing up, and I continued
them until the beloved Higher Power broke through and
showed me that my tenacious hold on the past was killing me.
Being an Adult Child Mourner, once I recognized the reality
of what had to be changed, I wanted it changed yesterday. I
had a hard lesson to learn — patience. After the long time it
took for me to come to terms with the need for change, I had
to give myself time to do the work. Intellectualizing was relatively easy. All the changes were up in my head. The beauty
of endings and beginnings was that wonderful word, that
magnificent feeling — *hope*. I learned, too, that after the initial
fear of changing and knowing that people around me wouldn't
like it, the lifting of the levels of denial became exciting.

Looking at the behaviors that had caused me such crippling
pain in destructive relationships all of my life was the beginning. I didn't want to feel that way anymore. I no longer
wanted to accept crumbs. Seeing what I did not want started
a chain of thought processes and memories. Some of my

denial had centered on my two sons. I began to recall that both of them had told me to "follow my path." (Actually what they said was, "Mum, you have such an amazing potential. Stop worrying about us and shit or get off the pot!")

That was seven years ago and here I am, just completing the order! I will be eternally grateful to both Colin and Daniel for the risk they took at that time.

So now it is necessary to look at the process for change.

Some of us think there is going to be one ending and that's it, but that's not the case. Life is like a jigsaw puzzle. One doesn't throw the pieces out on the board and put the whole puzzle together at once. It's one piece at a time. That's what endings are. There will be endings and there will be beginnings — always. Some people are as afraid of death as they are of life. That's sad because life and death are inevitable. It's nature. I have learned recognition of the power and the beauty of nature.

Things are born and things die every day of our lives — ideas, philosophies, our creativities at birth, things that are really crucially important to us. As we grow and change, sometimes we lose people along the road. Not by death, but because we outgrow them and we can't relate anymore. It's important to understand that's a healthy part of living.

The Prison Experience

A couple of years ago they built a new prison in Bucks County, Pennsylvania and invited those of us who'd worked in the prison system to stay overnight. Nice! It was a brand new prison. It was fun. I really cracked up at supper time when the judge standing behind me in line saw the men serving the meal. She said, "My God, I sentenced that one."

I said, "Let me get your meal for you, Judge."

It was interesting watching the behavior. The judges were really nervous about being locked up. They wanted out of there and some of them did in fact leave. I was enjoying it. I thought, "This is an experience." I like to experience things.

I don't go to school to learn; I put myself through treatment. I found out a whole lot about me.

I went to this prison thing and didn't care what happened. You know, *I was going to get out in the morning.* What did it matter to me? At that particular time the women were put in one section and then they brought the men in. Of course we behaved as we thought woman prisoners are supposed to. We whooped. We hollered. We howled. We whistled. They liked that.

Anyway, I was locked in this nice pale blue cell and I didn't care because *I was getting out in the morning.* Then I tried to go to the bathroom. Well, these people kept walking by and looking in — and have your ever tried to balance on a toilet while holding towels all around you? You know someone's going to peer in at you any minute. I didn't like that too much. But I still knew *I was getting out in the morning* and I didn't worry.

I sleep in a king-size bed at home and here I was in a cot. So I was hanging on for dear life but I thought it was funny. *I was getting out in the morning.* I didn't have to worry about a thing. Then the storm started. It hit something on the roof and made a tremendous noise. I remembered having seen some of the guards trying to open some of the cell doors in the prison earlier in the day. Some locks had jammed. I lay there and suddenly began to think. I first thought of my oldest daughter who had gone for an interview that day and I didn't know how it had gone.

The noise of the storm was horrendous. I remembered my second daughter who was terrified of storms. My oldest son had just left for California that morning, so my youngest son was going back to the house alone. I couldn't find out how they were. I couldn't get to a phone. At that time I realized and felt how a prisoner felt. Up to that time it had all been a joke. I learned to experience this and use it. It was extremely important to me to be able to understand how, when people come out of the prison system, they have no endings and they have very few new beginnings.

Beginnings and endings are simply transitions, and most people need help with them. I certainly do. I could never have done it alone.

So everything that the Higher Power has given me to experience has made me understand more. The understanding is critical in helping people through this transition. I don't necessarily need to know how they feel, but I need to understand.

In my own recovery I've taken a look at this word called choice. Really, we do have a choice. It's the old story of the glass half empty or half full — whichever way you want to look at it. But the choice is, as Viktor Frankl says, "A matter of conscience about yourself."

Each day is a new beginning — that's important and it's real. We have so many people telling us what to do, but the point is that *we have that choice*. Sometimes that choice is more difficult and more uncomfortable than staying where we are. It is important to move on.

When I look back on my life and the things that have happened to me, I'm not sure what I would have done had I known when I was ten years old what I was going to go through. I'm just not sure. More and more I'm beginning to understand why — thank God — up to now I've been able to deal with whatever's been given to me. It was in spite of a very important thing that got in my way — pride. I didn't need any help. I didn't need anybody. I could do it myself! What I did was overcome that pride and reach out and say to people, "I can't do this, would you please help me?"

It's so important to let significant people know that we are vulnerable. Yes, some of us have radio shows. Some of us own businesses. Some of us are world-famous. But we are people and we hurt and bleed like any other person. If I'm stabbed, I'm going to die like anybody else. It's important never, ever to forget that.

Humility

I love the word humility. I had to learn what it meant because I thought it was humiliation and my stepfather knew how to do that to me very well. Whether I'm dealing with a bank executive who puts his salary up his nose or I'm drag-

ging someone out of a gutter, those people have a personal
dignity that is crucial to their recovery. I don't care who they
are. As long as they are breathing, they have dignity.

A little while ago I went to Bill W.'s grave. I thought there
would be trumpets and flags and neon signs saying "Founder
of AA." I couldn't find it. I couldn't find his grave. I looked and
looked and finally found this ordinary grave with a headstone
that said his name, date of birth and date of death. At the foot
of the grave was a brass plaque that talked about his Army
career in World War I. That was all. Except by the headstone
there were a lot of buttons, coins and paper. I was down on my
knees and looked at that as such a lesson in humility. I was
utterly overwhelmed. My feelings and definition of humility
changed right there. Right then. I brought it back with me. I
was able to go to my groups and talk much more openly,
much more freely, able to give and share in a way I never had
before. Because who I am and what I do doesn't really matter.
It's the fact that I am here on this planet for a reason. We all are.

I was given two gifts for which I will be eternally grateful
to my Higher Power. One was the ability to deal with people
in extraordinary pain. The other was to be able to laugh with
myself. Not to deride myself as I did in the past with destructive humor, but to love my humor and use it constructively to
the best of my ability. It starts with me. It starts with all of us.

These things happen on a day-to-day basis — beginnings
and endings. The new beginnings are so exciting. You're never,
ever too old to do anything. I don't care how well versed I am
in my work or my growth as a woman. I will never be too
knowledgeable to learn. I have to learn on a day-to-day basis.

We were raised in a culture that says if you like yourself,
you're bragging, you're boasting. That's not true. I pray every
day — twice a day — "Please let me love myself as You love
me and let me go on." When you begin to love yourself and
trust yourself, other people do the same. I remember when I
was really sick, I would always look at other people and say,
"I'm as good as them. Why aren't I doing that?" I kept myself
in my own emotional prison, living the grief I had as a child.

When I learned to do visualization and imagery, I began to
release myself. I would actually see that I could let go. That I

could laugh and maybe be a little irreverent. So what? It doesn't really matter. When I was sick, I wanted everyone to behave the way I wanted them to behave so I would be comfortable. My children had to be very well-mannered. Very well-behaved. Heaven help them if they weren't.

I think it was Bob Ackerman who said something about "We never wanted to be like our parents." I did everything I could not to be like my mother, whom I thought I loved very much. My mother would never get up in the morning. I had to get three buses to get to school, but I took her a cup of tea in the morning and heaven help me if I didn't. So naturally, as a parent, what do you think I did? I got up for breakfast every morning with my children and I packed them a lunch and I made sure they were fed and so on.

One morning about a year ago all four of them were around for a brunch. I came down the stairs and heard my two sons talking to their sisters and saying:

"Do you remember when we used to pray that she wouldn't wake up? She'd come down in the morning:

'Would you like some toast?' 'How about some tea?' 'I made you muffins. 'I've made your lunch for you.'"

Well, I knew they ditched the lunches and bought cheese doodles, but I was being the perfect mother. I mean up to 12th grade I was trying to force tea and toast down my younger son. He was throwing up. I thought he had school phobia. It was me. He was throwing up over his mother. Poor soul.

Perfectionism

I just did everything different because I thought that was the right thing to do. The right thing was everything opposite to my mother — the other extreme. Crazy things like that. It's great to be able to be free. That's the other side of endings and beginnings. I don't have to be the perfect professional. I don't have to be the perfect woman. What a relief!

If you are still suffering from being perfect, take it from the imperfect one here — it is such a relief. It's like Atlas throwing the world off his shoulders. Just to really have a break and know that you are merely mortal. It is so great just to say, "I made a mistake," and not drop over because at one time I could never make a mistake. It was just too scary.

All the years that I was in and out of therapy, in and out of the program, I was not willing to make the change I had to make in order to live the life I had to live. I was not ready to do what I needed to do to be free from my past, not regaining my childhood, but living it fully for the first time.

For those of you who are struggling with being loved, open up your heart. I have some patients sometimes that I'd like to cut right through and just open them up and get my hand in there because they are in such pain.

The beauty of recognizing who you are will define your endings and your beginnings. Understand that both of those things are growth processes. Many times my inflexibility has landed me in dire straits. I've learned that flexibility and positive humor are the things that lead me through life in terms of my living, working and being with the Higher Power who guides me at all times.

Changing

Change is a dirty word for a lot of us. But accepting that change is what life is all about lets us use its power. Putting the changes into action is traumatic at first. We don't know which way to go. We need to ask for help. "Can I have a hug?" "Will you hold my hand?" and, "Will you help me through this because I don't know how to do it?" This is courage and bravery.

One night not long ago I sat in the car and asked, *"What has changed?"* I sat and asked for some help, some direction. The old fears arose. Having now acknowledged real love in my life, which I was no longer sabotaging, what did I want? Was it not going to be enough? I had heard about those Adult Child Mourners whose appetites for security were insatiable, and I did not want to be one of those people.

Suddenly — and I mean suddenly — it became crystal clear. I had nothing left to grieve! I was grieving the loss of childhood grief. There was nothing, no one to blame. I had grown up. All those years of therapy, treatment and self-help fellowship were paying off. The sudden realization of being an adult hit me with an enormous impact. "To Thine Own Self Be True" became an instant reality, rather like a 40-year overnight success!

Fear and relief battled on in me. Relief won and in that victory was forgiveness, gratitude, love and self-acceptance. Now I know the following are true about me:

- I can agree to disagree.
- I have accepted intimacy in my life.
- I practice rigorous honesty.
- I know when to be serious and when to be lighthearted.
- I have accepted myself, my character assets and defects, as being — *me.*
- I am not perfect.
- I make mistakes.
- I am human.
- I have fun.
- I have fallen in love.
- I take risks.
- I like my "occasional" arrogance.
- I have let go of my children (that was the hardest).
- I have accepted my intelligence (that wasn't too easy either!).
- I do not laugh if I don't want to.
- I laugh a lot.
- I take care of myself.
- I have vacations.
- I accept that "No" is a complete sentence.
- I embrace the 12-Step Program.
- I can be very silly.

And for the future? When I am older — that could be any time from now:

- I won't wear pantyhose.
- I'll wear loose garments and not hold in my stomach.
- I'll stop comparing myself to anyone other than myself.

- I'll stop making excuses because I lost myself in the middle of a sentence.
- I'll take a nap when I want one.
- I'll be irreverent if I am in the company of pompous asses.
- I'll giggle and play with my best friend, John, and I won't care when people say I am too old for "that sort of thing."
- I'll say no when I don't want to work with people who are phony.
- I'll be judgmental at times for my own good.
- I'll tell my children I love them whenever I want to, without it being an anniversary or something.
- I'll laugh when I want to and won't when I don't think it is funny.
- I'll say no to people who tell me their troubles but don't want to do the work it will take to get rid of them.
- I'll go to as many meetings as I choose to, maybe two or three a day or one every two weeks.
- I'll wear leg warmers of all bright colors.
- I'll wear hightop sneakers and elegant gowns whenever I choose (though I am not sophisticated enough to wear them at the same time).
- I *will eat ice cream* — not too much, but enough to feel like a child.
- I will buy a sports car even when I am told it's crazy (that's a good enough reason right there!).
- I'll go and talk with the ocean.
- I'll answer the question "Why?" with "Because."
- I'll send myself flowers and write a loving card.
- I'll write from my soul with no editing.
- My clothes will be bright yellows, peaches, pinks, blues and greens, and maybe I'll let my hair grow.
- I'll skip through meadows.
- I'll be naughty with the grandchildren.
- I'll get into trouble for doing what I could never do as a little child.

For this is my first childhood! I'll do all this as I get older, which could be any time from now.

I knew I had come full circle by my hair. It's a symbol for me. When I was little, I had very curly hair. From approximately the age of 12 I started straightening it — I pulled it, ironed it, wrapped it and struggled to manage it. As I got older it became easier, so my hair would always look well managed, sleek and coiffed. After leaving treatment a few years ago, I went to a new hairdresser for a haircut. The tall young woman said, "You've got naturally curly hair."

"How observant," I silently sneered and said, "Straighten it."

"I don't think so," she said.

I was horrified. "I don't like it curly."

"Let's just try it," she said, and before I knew it — snip, snip, snip. One doesn't argue with a person holding very sharp scissors in her hand!

I went home — curly, angry and scared. My sons were funny and compassionate, my daughter loved it. It took months for me to get used to it. I took out photographs of myself as a child and told the little girl how much I loved her, how pretty she was and especially what lovely curly hair she had.

After a while I went to a conference. A friend I hadn't seen in a while came over and said, "That's a great perm you've got there." I pulled myself up to my full height and said, "It's not a perm — it's really me!"

From that moment it all became so clear. I had resented my childhood so much that I wanted *no* reminder of it, not even my hair. It is a full circle now. I love my hair curly and short as opposed to long and straight. "Easy does it" certainly applies — it looks the same and gives me balance, forgiveness, acceptance and the love of the child within.

Reality

This last chapter may come as a shock to you. I believe a book of this nature must express the author's honesty and reality. Self-disclosure has never been a problem for me, even though I have endured a couple of attempted character assassinations. What I have learned in this regard is that most people exhibit this kind of malice only when the person they wish to control denies them the opportunity. So be it. I prefer it this way rather than once more to be in an emotional prison. This is called Recovery.

I recall an old rhyme: "Sticks and stones may break my bones, but names will never harm me." As a child, names did hurt. As a recovered Adult Child Mourner, they are water drops rolling off the proverbial duck's back.

This preamble then, is to prepare you for something a little different in terms of closure. Many people support peace-making techniques with families of origin. They advocate total forgiveness and creating a new "tone" relationship with them. If you can do that without losing all you have gained, I support it wholeheartedly. As Adult Child Mourners, however, we have had to recover from severe trauma. Not all of our stories can end glowingly. Some relationships with family of origin are simply unredeemable. They belong in "People, Places and Things" and are better left alone.

There's more than one way to go on with your life in happiness, excitement, health and serenity. The bottom line is letting go of the past, recognizing the grief and transforming all that pain, anguish and low self-esteem into healing.

In writing this book I have experienced much sorrow and much joy. Tremendous optimism has emerged as I have looked back. Speaking with others has given me strength. Teaching others has taught me. I have recalled incidents long suppressed in my little girl's unconscious. Recognition of why I had entered into such bizarre situations was made clear to me. What a relief to know:

- It wasn't my fault.
- I was not a bad child; I am not a bad person.
- Some people are sicker than others.
- Recovery is possible to whoever wants it.
- I have the right to . . .
      fun,
      happiness,
      love,
      success,
      money,
      excellent health
      and any fulfillment I choose.

I mentioned in a previous chapter that I enjoy a deep faith in a Higher Power, whom I choose to call God. My God has no sexual identity, so when I refer to this Higher Power as *it* I am not being disrespectful. I also believe in afterlife, alternate realities, mind over matter and other exciting possibilities. When I am stuck in my feelings or something seems out of control in my life and I can't handle it, I use automatic writing.

Automatic writing is a therapeutic tool in my recovery. I simply sit in a comfortable chair, close my eyes, relax and take several deep breaths. On my lap is a legal-sized pad, in my hand a writing implement that will not fade on me. I never know quite how long I'll be writing. When I first started this I just sat and wrote. After all these years I state a question and then await the results.

At first I write slowly. As I get into it, the pen flies over the paper. It gives me information that others perhaps get through meditation, and it pulls no punches. Usually it comes through my spirit guides. The information I am sharing in this book came from another source.

As I continue you will see the risk I am taking to publish this chapter. The decision to do so came from a Power greater than myself. This Power is a positive force in my life and is right in Its decisions.

Some people learn, grow and enjoy life through love, encouragement and joy. Others learn through adversity and come to know love, encouragement and joy. I have been in the second category most of my life. I am currently in the first, where I intend to remain one day at a time. I have grown through pain, grief and sorrow; learning, listening and accepting things I didn't want to know.

During the writing of this book, a strange phenomenon occurred. I took on — with a couple of notable exceptions — the personality, behavior and physical appearance of my mother. The exceptions are that I have a healthy relationship with a normal man, I have my own teeth, I work at what I like to do, I pray and have faith and I am not as obese as she was. However, in this writing I have put on close to 40 pounds.

As I felt this happening, my old feelings of helplessness arose. I didn't know what to do. I decided to work with colleagues on the parapsychology level to release me from emotional bondage. I had come as far as they could bring me, and now I was looking reality in the face. Rigorous honesty was called for and I wasn't sure that I had the strength for it. I knew that something was afoot. The question was, "How do I reach it?"

The more I thought about it, the more I realized that it concerned my relationship with my mother. I wanted to love her even though she had been dead for 27 years. I wanted to afford myself the opportunity to thoroughly recover from my Adult Child Mourning and settle things with her.

When I saw one of my colleagues recently, she told me that my mother was with me, had a message and would guide me for three months. I was heartily relieved. This was the chance I'd been waiting for. This was the total recovery for which I had yearned, an end finally to grieving the childhood that never was.

I have chosen to close this book with a series of letters and brief explanations between them.

It amazes me how tenacious the grieving child is in the first letter. She still wants beauty, peace, love and acceptance in the relationship. Although it was a true letter at the time of writing, it wasn't honest.

As you read on, take from the letters what you will. I cannot control your interpretation. For most of you still struggling to make your recovery from mourning work, this could be an option you have not considered. It's difficult and powerful, but then rigorous honesty always is.

A Letter To Cecelia, My Mother

Dear Cecelia,

I call you by your beautiful name because in a vision to Barbara Rose you asked me to. They called you *Cissie* — how sad. Most of your sisters had beautiful names, and those were mutilated too. It seemed that none of you were allowed to be who you were.

When I think of you, dear Cecelia, my heart is filled with sadness and compassion. How different it is from a few years ago when I despised the memory of you. I wrote a letter to you while I was in treatment, calling you pathetic, weak and unfulfilled. I raged against you and your marriage to Morris. You both stole my childhood.

There is so much mystery surrounding my conception, birth and very early childhood. As a perceptive woman, I know there must have been terrible pain for you to have to marry a most unattractive person to "give me a name." I have so many unanswerable questions. They haunted me for many years.

"Who was my father?"

"Why didn't you marry him?"

"Why did you put up with such abuse from your husband?"

"Why did you stay with him and send me away?"

"Why didn't you tell me about my birth?"

"Why didn't you ever support me in what I wanted to do with my life?"

None of these questions is relevant today. I have spent much time and energy screaming them out and now feel peace. When I tell my story people frequently ask, "How did you survive? Why aren't you bitter?"

Well, Cecelia, I went through all of that when I acknowledged your addiction, co-dependency and lower-than-low self-esteem. I felt pity for you, the most insulting of feelings. I didn't like that feeling. I felt anger, rage that you were so subservient, not only to your husband, but to your parents, brothers and sisters. Because of all that I was robbed of childhood. One day, Ceceilia, I am going to write that book about the family and your struggles with them. I owe you that.

My heart goes out to the memory of you, to the pain and agony of having no love in your life — at least the kind of which we all dream. I can only assume the depth of grief with which you had to live in a family which was steeped in complete denial. I don't think they could look at any situation with honesty and compassion.

The book is dedicated in part to you — my mother. I love you. Will you forgive me, as I have forgiven you? I have so much gratitude in me today because my spirituality has allowed me to grow and make the changes you couldn't make. I love in a healthy way now.

I often wonder what you would think if you saw me today. Maybe you do see me. I feel a presence at times, in my more spiritual moments. Certainly my life today is beyond my wildest dreams. At times I reflect on my childhood, youth, marriage, parenthood. I know that I had to experience all that occurred to be as I am today. Were it to be otherwise . . . well, that's an exercise in futility.

Cecelia, I would love you to know your grandchildren. Rosanne was five and Michelle 2½ when you died so young, so suddenly. I was seven months pregnant with Colin, and Daniel was born three years later. They know you. Your granddaughters have loving memories of you, and of course there are the photographs. My daughters talk of not having to finish their dinners and being fed sweets in bed with you. (If I didn't finish my meal — no dessert.) They have beautiful memories of you; my sons feel a little cheated. You would be so proud, Cecelia — they are fine men and women. And your great-grandchildren are gorgeous.

My Beloved Mother, I am so grateful to you. You taught me, in your pain, how to survive. As a parent myself, I now understand how excruciating it must have been to send me away without a word. I made many mistakes as a mother, and my children are luckier. They have me — alive. They can settle things with me, tell me how they feel about their childhood and lay pain, resentment and grief to rest. We can talk, laugh, argue, fight and love.

When I lecture now all over the United States, I talk to the symbol of my recovery — my hair. I have freed the curls and cut it short. Know what, Mum? It looks just like yours.

I love you, my mother Cecelia.

Be at peace.

Your daughter,
Yvonne

When I read this in retrospect, I can see how much my entire life depended on the acceptance and approval of others. I had to be kind, gentle and loving. It all had to be tied up so neatly. If the relationship wasn't as I wanted it to be, I created the illusion of what I wanted. Then I wrote the words that read the most poetic, bringing tears to the reader's eyes, letting them sigh with the perfect ending of it all.

Then I got real.

Letter To My Guides

I am getting very scared now. I seem to be my mother.

The lower part of my body is her on a smaller scale. My financial position and my jealousy of others in better shape or condition are just like her. The only thing I do have that she never had is a strong, reciprocal, loving, monogamous relationship with a good man. Please give guidance.

My Mother's Reply

You have sinned. Just as I did when you were conceived. It is not for women like us to know happiness, and you are being punished because you know happiness. The gods are angry that you took this man, and now you will receive nothing — no money, no work and you will grow fat and ugly. Inside you are lying to everybody. You will never be published because you are no good at anything, even writing the truth. You will be fat like me because you ruined my life. If it had not been for you, I would have been happy. Instead I had to live with that pig of a man to give you a name because I could not marry your father. I hated him. Why should I suffer alone? I do not accept your forgiveness. I do not forgive — why should I? You did nothing for me and I hate you for being as happy as you are now. You will get no help from me. Even though you were told I would help you, I will not. You do what you have to do. I will not lift a finger to help you. Why you were born, I'll never know. I wasn't sorry to send you away. It was a relief. Want to turn this around? Then you had better speak with your guides. I want nothing to do with you . . . Goodbye.

Second Letter To My Mother

Dear Mum,
What a disappointment. I thought we could resolve this terrible problem we have between us that has remained silent all these years. I didn't want to believe that you really hated me and blamed me for the unhappiness you had

with your marriage. I suppose I wanted to be loved so much by you that I tried to be just like you, even in your death. I just didn't want to face the truth. Because of the denial, I did not realize why I put so much weight on, why my earning capacity dropped, why my self-esteem took a dive. It wasn't simply that I wanted your love and approval — I became you. Almost.

Thank my Higher Power that I had the fortitude to withstand your passive/aggressive, guilt-producing influence. I am so grateful that I no longer have to have your approval to be alive and to be happy.

I do not hate you. Your anguish causes great sadness in me, but as a woman now I will not allow you to affect me any longer. I release you from my heart, my life and my soul. I pray for your peacefulness and hope you can now rest. As your message shows, you have at last told me the truth. I know you were incapable of being honest in life. Now you have been honest with me. Thank you. Perhaps my experience will help others who have been controlled from the grave to detach with love — of self.

It is indeed a tragedy that you suffered so terribly. It is very sad that I had to suffer, too, as a result of that pain and grief. I paid for your unhappiness with my childhood — a high price indeed. But no more. Definitely, *no more.*

I affirm myself as a beloved child of God and love myself as God loves me. I do not need that biological connection to a very sick, very unhappy woman.

Mum, you and I both know that I knew you better than anybody. What I had to do for you in your later years does not bear repeating. We both know and that is good enough.

In spite of you not accepting my forgiveness and my asking you to forgive me, I still forgive you. You have been forthright in your feelings towards me, and I can now let you go. Now I can concentrate on the people, places and things in my life that are positive, loving and accepting. I have not sinned. You did not either. The gods, as you call them, are not angry. That is just an excuse. Who is to judge anyway? Who wrote the rules?

Someone once said to me, "When it no longer matters, it will be all right." *It no longer matters.* I am grateful that you let me live, that you did what you could for me in whatever limited way was at your disposal. Now I have to take the steps to reverse the decisions I made to survive, so that my children will not be like I was. I have to break the cycle. And I do it like this:

God, grant me the serenity
To accept the things I cannot change,
Courage to change the things I can,
And the wisdom to know the difference.
Thy will, not mine, be done.

I feel such peace today, Mum. I pray for you to be a loving soul released from your feelings of hatred, revenge and rageful anger. If you can do what I am doing and release what your parents did to you, you will find the serenity and fulfillment I now have.

I have been taught in my recovery to use the gifts of humor and love. I offer these both to you. I know we will communicate again on a different level of peace and mutual respect — woman to woman, as I am doing with your granddaughters and grandsons today.

Yvonne

I struggled with this chapter because it will hurt some people who knew and loved my mother. To them I say, "Let your memories be your memories. Allow me my freedom."

This book has been cathartic to me, emphasizing how subtle adult child mourning can be. The level of denial has surprised me. When I started writing I thought I had dealt with it all. Now I know the depth of pain in the Adult Child Mourner and the beauty of Recovery.

The writings have brought more awareness to me, more for me to share with others on the journey. The most I have accomplished is a feeling of peace and self-acceptance.

"Whatever it takes." And — I lost the weight!!!

Tapestry Of A Woman

I am an emotional tapestry,
Created by the gifts of silken feelings
From those who have entered my life
And enriched it.

My core is formed from encounters with people
Who have loved me enough
To rearrange my thoughts
And show them to me.

I have learned from all those
Who have passed my way,
Experiences of all kinds,
Good and bad — nothing is wasted.

I have accepted the true meaning
Of life — for me.
I can give and I can take.
I can be wrong and I can be right.
I can be angry, happy, sad, funny, vulnerable,
Passionate and serene —
All those feelings flesh is heir to.

I can grieve and I can miss.
I can lose, but, of all things
I can love and so doing,

Create for those who have never known it.
A freedom that only deep love can bring.
I can only create if I am trusted
And that I have to earn . . . constantly.

—Yvonne Kaye

References And Sources

Lorna Helsinger — Summit Psychological Center, Feasterville.

"Soft is the Heart of a Child," Gerald T. Rogers. Operation Corks, Division of Kroc Foundation.

Why Am I Afraid To Tell You Who I Am? John Powell, S.J. Argus Communications, 1969.

Man's Search For Meaning, Viktor Frankl. Pocketbooks, 1959. (Simon and Schuster)

Elisabeth Kubler-Ross — Swiss born Psychiatrist/Thanatologist. **On Death And Dying,** Macmillan, 1970.

Thom Murgitroyde, CAC, CEAP — Director of Assistance Program AFL-CIO, Philadelphia/Interventionist.

The Water Babies, Charles Kingsley. (Pub. Vikas India) Advent, New York, 1983.

New Age Music — Relaxation.

Alcoholics Anonymous — 12-Step Program for Alcoholics.

12-Step Programs.

Caron Foundation Family Program, Wernersville, Pennsylvania.

Shalom Mountain — Jerry Judd. Livingston Manor, New York.

Parapsychology Alternate Solutions.

Yvonne Kaye, Ph.D., CCGC
22 North York Road, Willow Grove, PA 19090.
(215) 659-7110

Daily Affirmation Books from . . .
Health Communications

GENTLE REMINDERS FOR CO-DEPENDENTS: Daily Affirmations
Mitzi Chandler

With insight and humor, Mitzi Chandler takes the co-dependent and the adult child through the year. Gentle Reminders is for those in recovery who seek to enjoy the miracle each day brings.

ISBN 1-55874-020-1 $6.95

TIME FOR JOY: Daily Affirmations
Ruth Fishel

With quotations, thoughts and healing energizing affirmations these daily messages address the fears and imperfections of being human, guiding us through self-acceptance to a tangible peace and the place within where there is *time for joy.*

ISBN 0-932194-82-6 $6.95

AFFIRMATIONS FOR THE INNER CHILD
Rokelle Lerner

This book contains powerful messages and helpful suggestions aimed at adults who have unfinished childhood issues. By reading it daily we can end the cycle of suffering and move from pain into recovery.

ISBN 1-55874-045-6 $6.95

DAILY AFFIRMATIONS: For Adult Children of Alcoholics
Rokelle Lerner

Affirmations are a way to discover personal awareness, growth and spiritual potential, and self-regard. Reading this book gives us an opportunity to nurture ourselves, learn who we are and what we want to become.

ISBN 0-932194-47-3
(Little Red Book) $6.95
(New Cover Edition) $6.95

SOOTHING MOMENTS: Daily Meditations For Fast-Track Living
Bryan E. Robinson, Ph.D.

This is designed for those leading fast-paced and high-pressured lives who need time out each day to bring self-renewal, joy and serenity into their lives.

ISBN 1-55874-075-9 $6.95

3201 S.W. 15th Street,
Deerfield Beach, FL 33442-8190
1-800-851-9100

Health Communications, Inc.

New Books . . .
from Health Communications

ALTERNATIVE PATHWAYS TO HEALING: The Recovery Medicine Wheel
Kip Coggins, MSW
This book with its unique approach to recovery explains the concept of the
medicine wheel — and how you can learn to live in harmony with yourself,
with others and with the earth.

ISBN 1-55874-089-9   **$7.95**

UNDERSTANDING CO-DEPENDENCY
Sharon Wegscheider-Cruse, M.A., and Joseph R. Cruse, M.D.
The authors give us a basic understanding of co-dependency that everyone
can use — what it is, how it happens, who is affected by it and what can
be done for them.

ISBN 1-55874-077-5   **$7.95**

THE OTHER SIDE OF THE FAMILY:
A Book For Recovery From Abuse, Incest And Neglect
Ellen Ratner, Ed.M.
This workbook addresses the issues of the survivor — self-esteem, feelings,
defenses, grieving, relationships and sexuality — and goes beyond to help
them through the healing process.

ISBN 1-55874-110-0   **$13.95**

OVERCOMING PERFECTIONISM:
The Key To A Balanced Recovery
Ann W. Smith, M.S.
This book offers practical hints, together with a few lighthearted ones, as a
guide toward learning to "live in the middle." It invites you to let go of your
superhuman syndrome and find a balanced recovery.

ISBN 1-55874-111-9   **$8.95**

LEARNING TO SAY NO:
Establishing Healthy Boundaries
Carla Wills-Brandon, M.A.
If you grew up in a dysfunctional family, establishing boundaries is a
difficult and risky decision. Where do you draw the line? Learn to recognize
yourself as an individual who has the power to say no.

ISBN 1-55874-087-2   **$8.95**

3201 S.W. 15th Street,
Deerfield Beach, FL 33442-8190
1-800-851-9100

Health Communications, Inc.